You Never Know

A Memoir

Romy Shiller, Ph.D.

Trafford
PUBLISHING

*We at Trafford believe that it is the responsibility of us all, as both individuals
and corporations, to make choices that are environmentally and socially sound.
You, in turn, are supporting this responsible conduct each time you purchase a
Trafford book, or make use of our publishing services. To find out how you are
helping, please visit www.trafford.com/responsiblepublishing.html*

*Our mission is to efficiently provide the world's finest, most comprehensive
book publishing service, enabling every author to experience success.
To find out how to publish your book, your way, and have it available
worldwide, visit us online at www.trafford.com/10510*

www.trafford.com

North America & international
toll-free: 1 888 232 4444 (USA & Canada)
phone: 250 383 6864 ♦ fax: 250 383 6804
email: info@trafford.com

The United Kingdom & Europe
phone: +44 (0)1865 722 113 ♦ local rate: 0845 230 9601
facsimile: +44 (0)1865 722 868 ♦ email: info.uk@trafford.com

10 9 8 7 6 5 4 3 2

The people mentioned in this book should not be associated with my perspective. They may or may not agree with anything I have to say. The book contains my ideas alone.

For my mother

CONTENTS

7

Introduction

No Choice

OUR DEEPEST FEAR IS NOT THAT WE ARE INADEQUATE...
OUR DEEPEST FEAR IS THAT WE ARE POWERFUL BEYOND MEASURE.
IT IS OUR LIGHT, NOT OUR DARKNESS, THAT MOST FRIGHTENS US.
—Marianne Williamson

BELIEVE NOTHING, NO MATTER WHERE YOU READ IT, OR WHO
SAID IT, NO MATTER IF I HAVE SAID IT, UNLESS IT AGREES WITH
YOUR OWN REASON AND YOUR OWN COMMON SENSE.
—Buddha

WHAT YOU ARE about to read happened to me. I try to make no excuses. I am a big believer in personal responsibility. Did I choose to get a brain tumour? No, I did not. But I did react to it. I am pretty sure it is an unconscious kind of thing.

They say I am a medical mystery or, some say, "miracle"; I was in a coma for five months. I did not speak from August 2003 until March 2004—even when I came out of the coma. The term is "akinetic mutism."

I really did not think of myself as a particularly happy person before the surgery. I am quite pleased with my response. On the whole, I was quite positive. I still am. I might get depressed in the future. If I do, I do. For now, I do not sit in dark corners, feel sorry for myself or take drugs. I laugh constantly. Maybe this is my disposition or constitution. Who knows? All I know is that I survived an ordeal of huge proportions, I am still surviving and, for many reasons, I am truly grateful.

This is not to say that physically I do not wish that I were back to the way I was. It would be so much easier on many levels.

It is very difficult for me to look in a mirror. In my mind's eye, I look (and sound) as I did before and, to be perfectly honest, I prefer that to what is in the mirror these days. It may be superficial, but that's how I feel. Of course, I can choose to see beauty on the inside, but it would seem I don't. That would be rational and even logical, especially at this point. So, you see, I know how difficult "choice" is.

So many people say I am an inspiration to them. I am conflicted about this because I never set out to be an inspiration. I did not cut off my own limb to save myself like that guy Aron Ralston did. I am no Lance Armstrong, who continues to inspire everyone who knows about him. They obviously did not set out to be inspirational, but they are. And in my opinion, they are mega fantastic.

I watched *Oprah* and saw two disabled guys who inspired me. As a result, I had a good dinner with my sister-in-law's dad, Bert, and his wife, Karen. They had not seen me since before the surgery. For me, watching this show was synchronistic. I made it personal, and it worked for me. I think awareness is key.

Anyhow, I have food in my belly and shelter over my head. For these reasons and more, I consider myself truly lucky. It is by no means easy, but at least I don't have to worry about the basics. If this had to happen, I am in pretty fortunate circumstances. I always feel encouraged; there seem to be many possibilities for me. This is a definite bonus.

I was never scared or frightened. I am still more interested in my condition than anything else. The interesting part was that I had very little or no control with regard to what happened. I had to give up the idea of control. This can be very liberating. It seems like I am a "glass is half full" - type of person. In any case, I really believe most of this stuff is intuitive. Like I said, maybe it is just my nature, but I simply felt this in my gut. I made the phone calls I had to make and I let nature take its course. This is not to say I was ever fatalistic—I asked many questions about my surgery—but I could do nothing about the tumour inside my brain. I had two lawyers help me with a living will and a will. You never know.

Weirdly enough, I also made plans in case I went into a coma. I assumed some part of me would "hear" stuff and I made my mom promise to read to me from my favourite book at the time and to play my music. She did. I remember nothing of this.

I am told I laughed or rasped appropriately at the punch lines of certain jokes at a time when I was still in the coma. I wish I could remember the jokes and the laughter, but I do not. Then again, I have a picture of myself at four years old at a birthday party I don't remember, at a house I don't remember. Even in late January, when I was out of the coma, there was an event that I absolutely have no memory of. Someone whom I know quite well came to visit me. Apparently I was quite vivacious at the time and I recognized her. So, for me, memory has little to do with consciousness. I was certainly perceptive at all these times, but the jury is still out on the specific meaning.

It is difficult for me to use a pencil or pen, so, in a sense, this book is my journal. It really never felt cathartic though; it was not a release, maybe because I am still dealing with my new physical repercussions. My handwriting is incredibly problematic now and my letters look very childish. In the very beginning of rehab, I could barely write by hand at all, so even this is an improvement. I really enjoy the process of writing, so the book was more of a compulsion—something I had to do and wanted to do. Maybe this book justifies what I went through and what I am still going through. In many respects, it hardly matters to me as long as it is beneficial and not detrimental to me.

I typed out my entire book using one bent finger. This was much slower than I am used to, and while it was a challenge, it did not feel daunting to me. I could really think about what I wanted to say because I had more time. I would get physically tired during this process, so I would stop and take breaks. I would do it again. Believe it or not, I simply would not let my present physical difficulties get in the way. I know it would have been very understandable just to stop; however, that is so unlike me. Also, outside of all the therapy I am doing, writing was a distraction. While my subject matter was about what I have to deal with now, there was a certain "project" aspect to it. I like projects.

Although what I went through was quite unique, my story was never a subject for a book—although, of course, it has become one. I continue to live the story and I could guess the ending, but I would rather leave it unfinished. To be quite honest, I prefer stories that are open-ended. I know this bugs many people who would prefer closure, things neatly wrapped up, but what can I say? That part of my story is not written yet. In my case, it would be very satisfying to know the end. But I do not. I know what I would like to happen. Whether it does or does not, only time will tell. These are the cards I have been dealt—like them or not.

I am glad that I can write this book, but I am a writer (amongst other things) so writing about what happened is second nature to me. I guess what I want you to know is that writing continues to be pleasurable to me. Even if I am not tickled about my physicality at present, at the very least there is that.

I do not have a loving and knowledgeable partner in life to mediate on my behalf medically, but I do have parents and brothers with a vested interest in my health and welfare. I feel so lucky to have them. They were, and are, a great resource to me. When I was in the hospital, they were all quite extraordinary. Faced with an imminent challenge, they really stepped up to the plate.

At times, I get ticked off. I am only human, after all. I do not want to be anyone's mission, yet I find I am often people's lesson. On an esoteric level, this is amazing; but on a physical level, I really don't appreciate it. I'm not a so-called guinea pig. Lessons are interesting notions. I feel we can learn things vis-à-vis other people or situations. If I get hurt, however, that's a different story. I have little tolerance for these kinds of mistakes. It becomes my lesson and I may not choose to participate any longer. For me, the idea of "choice" is a liberty I have here. Options are very good. The thing about esoteric lessons is how we choose to react to them. Personally, I love to see how this plays out in others. Sometimes I get quite disappointed, but this is about expectation, which I try to avoid. Expectations are so difficult to deal with: They are a major challenge.

I was pretty ambivalent about getting my Ph.D. Now I am glad I have it. I like being called Doctor, even though I am not a Doctor of Medicine. I learned a lot and I know it speaks to my dedication, stamina and skills in addition to my intelligence. Maybe I need this degree because of the preconceptions that go along with disability. It seems to stun people when they find out. I am more than willing to see rationalization in this now. I am so glad that I have this in my pocket, whatever the reasons I might use now. The degree is not only an identity, it is part of my personal evolution.

I know that I have incentive enough to try to recover. Reminders, though well intentioned, feel insulting. And I do try, but I am also painfully aware of my physical limits at present. I believe I will overcome most of these in the future. Whatever disability remains, I will deal with. For me, there is no alternative; there is no choice. In addition to the earlier incidences, what you are about to read is where I am now.

Chapter 1

Why Not?

SOME MEN SEE THINGS AS THEY ARE AND SAY, "WHY?" I DREAM
OF THINGS THAT NEVER WERE AND SAY, "WHY NOT?"
—George Bernard Shaw

MISTAKES ARE THE PORTALS OF DISCOVERY.
—James Joyce

AUGUST 13, 2003 - I get to start all over again. So my brother Warren says. I say it puts a whole new spin on reincarnation—if you believe in that sort of thing. I am still me, with a new physical twist. I mean, babies are the same people until they get old; their bodies truly alter. Actually, we all change bodies several times in a lifetime, don't we? Take gaining or losing weight to changes over time, like aging or wrinkles. Sometimes we expect the changes and sometimes we do not. I never expected this.

When I was not speaking, I was never bothered or worried. I think this facet of my new reality was much harder on those around me, like my family and friends.

When I did start to talk, it was very difficult to communicate what I wanted. People had a hard time understanding me. This was incredibly frustrating, to say the least. I remember that I wanted a certain medication I used to take to clear my sinuses. I asked some nurses for it, but they had a difficult time making out my request. They finally got what I said, but I had to do a lot of repeating.

The coma is a total blank to me. People came and went, but I have no memory of it at all. Much of what I learned about the coma, I learned later. This spans the emotional content felt by those around me to the actual physical component of what my body was going through at that time. My gist is that the coma allowed my brain some time to heal. Although I continue to recover, the initial stuff is done with.

I don't remember much from that entire time, but I remember my dreams. There is nothing else to call them but dreams. They were so much more than lifelike. I recall that I changed nationalities in most of them. And many of them were set in nature. There were forests, sandy beaches and water. They were so colourful and odd.

In the first dream, *I dreamt that I was having a hair transplant in a M*A*S*H-like tent. It was incredibly industrial. I was moved outside, where it was snowing, to another "tent." I became black (in this reality, I am white and Jewish) then I became Asian. My brother Warren became black and my brother Doug became Asian.*

What a weird dream! Why not? In reality, I was having a drain replacement in my head. That's right; I had brain surgery three days before. When they replaced the drain, I remember that I was cold and that I met the nurses. A doctor, the one who would do the drain replacement, introduced himself to me. He had just come out of another surgery, the nurses said, and I remember thinking he must be tired. It was three or four o'clock on a Saturday morning. A different neurosurgeon had to do emergency surgery later on because there was some unexpected bleeding in my brain—yuck and "oy." It is very odd to me, because I do have memories of the drain episode and then nothing. This neurosurgeon said there may have been a venous system injury during the initial surgery, so while my brain looked for another route for the blood to return, it caused dysfunction and hence a coma, but that is a guess.

It was as if there was a glass wall between me and the world until late 2006, so I really could not articulate my concerns or questions for a very long time. I knew that something was wrong and that there were big differences, but the specifics were much harder to organize. I was absolutely able to discuss certain issues and implications, but something was lacking. Additionally, I have a major voice and speech impediment (even though I did not have a stroke, I sound like I did). There are some people I just won't talk to. I work on this issue with my speech pathologist, Tamara. She is so reassuring, but to be quite honest, I don't know what to think now. I would really like to think the best of everyone, but I am currently maybe permanently disabled.

I do not know definitively what happened to me. I will just have to deal with my physicality no matter what. You do not have to be a genius to figure out that there must be a link between the bleeding in my brain, the coma, etc. Accidents happen, and if one happened to me, it has changed my life. I have no proof of any wrongdoing; I just have some memories that make me suspicious. My wish is that people in the know were more forthcoming, but I won't hold my breath. The way I see it, I might be too kind but I am certainly not naive. This result was not the intention. Similarly, the risks were not made known to me. In fact, I was told I would be back at work at the maximum in fifteen weeks. Man, were they wrong! Whatever happened happened, despite people's professional intent. It may be strange, but I am probably the least mad or resentful person this could happen to.

On to other things…

I ask a lot of questions, and the meaning depends on the listener. I happen to be a person who prefers to be informed. I am pretty straightforward, but I don't want to hurt people's feelings, so I avoid certain topics. Maybe this is a flaw. I do not think I am as "in your face" as I could be. I am thinking of one individual in particular who is like this, and many people I know fit into this category. I don't do this, so in a way, my experience is vicarious. A point can certainly be made in this manner, but I prefer to use other means. In any and all cases, what I intend to get across does get delivered. To me, it boils down to a question of comfort and style. Sometimes what we do offends others, but what can we do about it? We all cannot be mind readers, and others' reactions, I believe, say more about who they are anyways. As long as no one gets hurt either way, why not? I mean, debate teams are specifically set up to have opposite points of view. Opposition does not have to be a bad thing. How is that for a concept?

I know drag queens and I know men who have gotten married—to each other. To me, this is usual, but I know for many people it is not. They fight for what they believe in.

How they "appear" or how they act is synchronous with their message, whether this is their intention or not. How they are "read" or interpreted depends on the attitude of the one "reading." My feeling is that it is about integrity. Whether they encounter opposition or derision, they carry on. I value that. Confronted by opposing points of view, they continue living their lives. To me, they are an inspiration, to say the least. I am more than glad they are an influencing factor in my life and in my way of thinking.

You know, I once performed with *The Greater Toronto Drag King Society*. I am female and I did female drag to show that even members of the same "sex" can learn this behaviour. While a lot of it was research for my doctoral dissertation, I was surrounded by fabulous people and it was an amazing experience. This might seem strange to many people, but I am so glad I did it. To me, drag is about manifesting a difference. It is not about crossing over to play an "other," often what we perceive as our opposite, as is usual in cross-dressing. Drag can be about putting on clothes, but it doesn't have to be about that.

I call what I am experiencing now "disability drag." This idea might irk some people. I am sure many cannot wrap their lovely heads around this. If you belong to this group, you are not alone. I know people who cross-dress and perform drag yet just do not get it. Some may think I am making light of the situation I am in. I am not. Some may think this is radical, considering the state of things now.

I am very conscious of my representation. In a familiar way, I am not crossing over to anything. I am not donning or putting on anything. I am, however, manifesting a dif-

ference. Likewise, I cannot take this disability off. Before, I
could walk, talk and sound like people expected. My physicality is very different now.

I am manifesting a difference. It is my strong belief that
everyone, especially people with disabilities, needs to rethink
the body. This might seem radical and it requires lots of courage, but it's worth it. First of all, people are not "trapped"
by their bodies. Although it might feel like it, a person will
adapt and find ways of doing things. Naturally, there is a
feeling of limitation when you are disabled. Dependency and
asking for help is tough. This world is built for able bodies.
There is a presumption that everyone is the same. Everyone
is not the same.

Differences can be very scary to many people when the
goal has always been to fit in, to assimilate. Bodies are supposed to look a certain way. Industries are set up to reinforce
that belief, like the beauty sector, gyms and diets, etc. Mark
Twain once said, "Be careful about reading health books. You
may die of a misprint."[1] We need to reassess what the body
actually means. This involves two major processes: mental-
ity and physicality. In my opinion, both are intertwined. We
have ideas about the body, right? Personally, I do not think
there is an "inside" and "outside." To me, this idea is a convention. I understand the impulse behind it, but I don't buy
into it. This major issue has been dealt with by academics, so
I will not presume to repeat it now. I know this idea might
be confusing to many people, but I believe the body is more
fluid than that. There is more of a relationship between the

---

1   < http://www.quotedb.com/quotes/668>

so-called "inside" and "outside" than we generally allow for.

Interestingly, most of my academic focus before this happened had to do with the body. In many ways, I feel prepared for this. I do not think you need to study this stuff in order to "get it." I am just saying it has helped me. It is incredibly synchronous that this happened to me. My body has become an example of my work and belief system. To me, this is a blessing. I may not like my physicality, but I am not conflicted by it.

Drag is about layering codes. Codes can be pretty much anything, but they suggest dominant belief structures, in my analysis. My feeling is that drag plays with these codes and "subverts" them. I do not believe drag has to be about clothing, but it often is. Clothing can be an awesome marker of gender. I believe we have to revise the meaning for man, woman, gender, sexuality and species, just to name a few. To me, "identity" is about expressing oneself, and drag seems to articulate this. Many people assume sexuality is aligned with drag. It can be, but I do not believe it has to be.

People use the expression of being trapped in a body. The body, to me, is fluid. Likewise, I feel there is a blur to most categories and definitions, including sexuality. Most everything is on a spectrum. Some people identify with a category strongly. There is no right or wrong in all of this, but it is necessary to look at the role ideology plays.

Okay, so I call what I am experiencing now "disability drag." I am not putting anything on, but I am manifesting a huge difference. Aside from not being able to walk, I have poor vision. I see a low-vision specialist and I have not read a book since my surgery. I cannot write by hand, so signing my name is incredibly problematic. I speak so differently now; I do not sound like I used to. I do not sing, and singing had been an important part of my life. The left side of my face does not move. The entire left side of my body is so different than the right. Using my left arm and hand is nearly impossible. I have not sucked on a mint or candy or chewed gum in a long while. There is some food I just will not eat for fear of choking. I cannot dance—the energy between Jamie (who died) and I when we danced together was astounding (I write about him in chapter 5). I cannot swim—once I was on a swim team. I cannot whistle. I cannot clap. The limitations of my body are substantial. I could feel very sorry for myself. While I would like things to be different, they are not. This is my life, like it or not. I don't think many people could handle my current physicality. I feel very strong mentally. My body seems to belie that. The issue of control is compelling. I have no control over my physical limitations, yet I feel very much in control of myself. There is a dichotomy, a straddling effect. Anyone trying to put me in a "box" or category is going to be surprised. I am an anomaly.

To me, living on the fringe is truly comfortable. I am now on the border of most everything. In a very lucky way, I can intellectualize my situation. I definitely have issues—everyone does. When people feel sorry for me, my feeling is they probably don't understand where I am coming from. Pity does not work for me; compassion on the other hand is totally acceptable.

There are lots of presumptions when it comes to disability. My identity has inadvertently changed. I enjoy playing with preconceived notions. For instance, it stuns many people that I have a Ph.D. The fact that I used to act and look differently really bothers a lot of people. I have few issues with my current physicality; others seem to have more. My current physical status is a doozy. It's quite the challenge, but I have a unique opportunity here to explain what I mean by "drag." Believe it or not, this can be viewed in a positive light. My current physicality resonates with many of my interests. I am very willing to use my situation. I do not feel that this is exploitative; it is realistic. It is also how I cope. I use my situation, but I did not ask for it nor would I have chosen it.

Drag is resistance to societal norms. It is an effective way to make a point. Most do not recognize that they are doing this. They really do not need to—what they signify is important. It also helps if they are read appropriately. I like that drag shakes things up. It foregrounds expectation and presumption. It resists dominant forms of being. It is quite radical. Whether you like it or not, it puts things we take for granted into question.

Difference is something that most people avoid. Fitting in becomes a goal. Personally, I think difference is valuable. It's the "same" that irks me. Variation is not the same as inconsistency. One can be incredibly multi-tonal and consistent. That's what I mean by "layered."

Drag intervenes with identity. Gender seems to be a focus, and is the object of my discussion in my thesis, but many identities would be effective tools for discussion and exploration. For instance, I have a permanent shunt in my head to drain excess fluid off my brain. I am taken out of the realm of being human into a new world occupying cyber territory. I am now a cyborg. To me, this is "cyborg drag." As before, I did not ask for this but I do have it. I'm not making light of my situation by calling it drag. The confusion arises because "drag" is often considered silly. It is serious to me. The idea of foregrounding identities by practical means is substantial. It is critical.

Penelope Cruz (a Spanish actor) has said, "He can have my body, but he will never have my soul. Never!"[2]

The body is full of meaning placed upon it by culture, by ideology. Meaning can change. Imagine the change around us if we related to our bodies differently than was expected. This can substantially affect mood, for one. Expectation shifts, presumption transforms. The body is so malleable; some would say fragile. It might feel broken to some, but believe it or not, several people have an opportunity to create a mini revolution. Che Guevara ("an Argentine-born Marxist revolutionary, political figure, and leader of Cuban and internationalist guerrillas.")[3] once said, "Many will call me an adventurer—and that I am, only one of a different sort: one of those who risks his skin to prove his platitudes."[4] I feel we are all adventurers.

Realistically, your thoughts, words and/or acts can make a huge difference. Creating a new reality for yourself and those around you is possible. This is not hocus-pocus. It does not require any ability other than will and determination.

2 See ThinkExist.com, <http://thinkexist.com/quotes/sent-by/tequisia69>

3 See <http://en.wikipedia.org/wiki/Che_Guevara>

4 <http://www.brainyquote.com>

Action does not need to involve movement. John Bradshaw (John Bradshaw is called "America's leading personal growth expert."[5] said, "IT'S ESSENTIAL TO TELL THE TRUTH AT ALL TIMES. THIS WILL REDUCE LIFE'S PAIN. LYING DISTORTS REALITY. ALL FORMS OF DISTORTED THINKING MUST BE CORRECTED."[6] We need to tell our truth and we need to reshape our thoughts.

It is possible to be textured or layered and be consistent. I believe these aspects exist in most of us harmoniously.

I am trying to recover. I am trying to return to the way I was. What we do or how we think might be contrary to others' belief systems, but I believe that it is important to persevere, to follow your heart.

---

5   See <http://www.creativegrowth.com/johnbio.htm>
6   <http://en.thinkexist.com>

Chapter 2

Sure

THE TUMOUR WAS pretty big and it was located in the fourth ventricle. That is, it was in the back of the head, near the brain stem. It is officially called a "choroid plexus papilloma." I had some decidedly bad symptoms: I think of them as "events." First (and one time only), I could not see half of my face in a mirror and my hearing was wonky. Then, a few weeks before the first surgery, I threw up. I spent the entire day in bed, which I never do, thinking I had a migraine headache or sinus infection. Sure.

Right before the first surgery, I went to Montreal, where I grew up. I saw my brothers, Warren and Doug, my brother Doug's wife, Sonya, and my long-time friend, Joy. I used to imagine I would return to Montreal to live. My fantasy included having a loft on the Lachine Canal, which is on the water, right near the Atwater Market, full of fresh flowers—a place I absolutely adore. That is where I had had brunch with the gang. Even though I was not feeling well, I did eat some good food. I took sinus medication at the restaurant thinking it might help or at least alleviate my symptoms. We took a picture on a bridge over the Lachine Canal. It is now by my bed and I look at it every day.

I made the decision to wait until I got back to Toronto to see a doctor. I called my family doctor, but she was away, so I spoke to the doctor on call. I described my symptoms and told her I thought it was a migraine. She said that what I was describing did not sound like that and I should go to an emergency room. This call and decision changed my life. I immediately called my boss to let her know I might not be in at work the next day. Little did I know I would never be back. She offered to drive me to the hospital, but I declined. That was so thoughtful and generous; however, I decided to walk there alone.

In addition to the tumour, or because of it, I had hydrocephalus, so they put me on cortisone to stop the brain from swelling. The fluid that goes from your spine to "bathe" the brain was not circulating properly. Surgery was the only option.

My general practitioner came to visit me in the hospital before and after the coma. I always really liked her and was immensely glad to see her. I heard that she had been very upset at my condition, but she was fine around me. Incredibly professional, I thought.

I remember her telling me that her own family, like mine, had a hard time gaining access to a hospital to see her ill dad because of the raging SARS epidemic. It made the experience of access quite universal for me. In addition, I was completely unaware of everyone's difficulty in this matter.

SARS was such a big thing in Toronto. Everybody I knew was terrified of getting it. There was a big demand for face masks. Ill persons were suspect. Contact with others was limited. One woman at work quarantined herself for ten days because she might have been exposed to the virus. I thought this was very prudent of her. I completely understand the hospital's reticence to let people in. They would not know who was infected with the virus or who was bringing it into the hospital. There were special stations set up where people could sanitize their hands without water. This lasted for a considerable length of time.

A while back, I did some research on this (or a similar sanitizing product) for a public relations firm. I looked at 2,000 years of hand washing history. To say I learned something is an understatement. I carry my new knowledge with me everywhere. Did you know that many adults and babies died from simple germs on their hands before hand washing was readily available? In any case, it gave a broader meaning to what the hospital was doing.

A surgeon said I had fluid and swelling near the brain stem post-surgery. Also, there was a mysterious white substance released that nobody has been able to identify to this day. The doctors initially said that I would recover from the surgery. No one expected me to go into a coma. I was supposed to feel like someone hit the back of my head with a baseball bat and I was going to walk like a "drunken sailor" for a while. Yup. Now I feel "drunk" all of the time. Imagine how that feels. Unfortunately, I cannot stop drinking to fix this. Again, this is something I have no control over.

The brain tumour was unique from the get-go. Usually only young children get this type of tumour, and here I was, not a young child but an adult. It was 2003 when I walked into the hospital. I have not walked since.

I asked the doctors tons of questions about my impending surgery and condition. I did not question whether I would have the surgery. I was fully aware that I really needed it and I am more than grateful to most of the doctors who I believe saved my life. I would have appreciated knowing what "dysarthria" is, a voice and speech impediment that I now have. I really like knowledge; I prefer to be in the loop. Naturally, I did not know the term "dysarthria" and condition or I would have asked about it. I think patients need to know more about what might happen. Now I am all for optimism—pessimism really bugs me—but I do like to know the "what ifs." Unfortunately, these never came my way. Not that it would have changed anything, but I would have liked to know. There are some people who prefer to remain in the dark. I am not one of those people. A friend once asked me if I would want to be told if I was being cheated on. It would be unpleasant (to say the least), but I would rather know. Knowledge works for me.

I had what I consider five initial surgeries. The first, eight hour most humongous one was to remove the tumour and check it for cancer. The second was a drain replacement, after which I do not remember anything until after the coma, except for my dreams. The third was an emergency to correct some bleeding in my brain. Then I had another drain replacement. During the fifth, my drain was replaced with a permanent shunt.

My initial surgery was postponed for two days. I did not want to get too hungry, because they would not let me eat before the planned surgery, so I asked my brothers to get me spaghetti and a strawberry milkshake from a restaurant I used to frequent quite a bit. I also thought that maybe this would be my last supper. In a way, it was: I had a feeding tube for eleven months, there are some things I will not eat now and I am not the same physically.

The morning of the surgery, I did ballet steps. I find it ironic that I cannot walk now. My balance and coordination are so off. I was also in great shape. I went to the gym a minimum three times per week. I did the Stairmaster˚—I called it the stair mistress—for 45 minutes and I swam. I also took a multivitamin and a vitamin C supplement every day. In many ways, I guess my body was prepared for surgery.

Chapter 3

Hurry Up And Wait

SICKNESS SHOWS US WHAT WE ARE.
Latin Proverb

REMEMBER THAT NOT GETTING WHAT YOU WANT IS SOMETIMES A
WONDERFUL STROKE OF LUCK.
—The Dalai Lama

RAIN! WHOSE SOFT ARCHITECTURAL HANDS HAVE POWER TO
CUT STONES, AND CHISEL TO SHAPES OF GRANDEUR THE VERY
MOUNTAINS.
—Henry Ward Beecher

I TELL PEOPLE that this is a life lesson. What have I learned? I have found out that I am much more resilient than I thought. When we are confronted by adversity, we really see what we are made up of. It is like a mirror held up to whom we really are. I think that "mirror" can be many different situations. We may think we know ourselves, but what a reality check. For me, it was very sudden, unexpected and completely unpremeditated. My initial reaction and continuing positivism constantly surprises me. If I think about it, I imagine I should be way more negative. But I have few, if any, regrets and I feel that my life has been quite interesting. I suppose that this is a part of it. People say I count my blessings. I guess I do.

I have also heard that I am afforded a second chance. Perhaps this is what I was supposed to experience during my lifetime. I feel like I had to grow up, to do certain things, to be able to express myself in certain ways—I had to be ready. What I do not think is understood is that this feels like an evolution to me. I have to put all I studied regarding "the body" into practice. What I learned is a kind of reflection of my present situation. For some reason, I make a relationship.

I now get the chance to look at my own internalized ideas about "the body." I know that many people would simply focus on their disabilities, so I am pleased I do this. There is a shift in my non-academic perspective on beauty, for instance. The way I look now has been a substantial issue for me. That this is one of my challenges feels synchronous and unbelievable.

My attitude seems very strange to many people around me, but I continue despite formidable opposition. I could be like most people expect—but I am simply not depressed or distraught about my condition. Many people see themselves in me. They gauge my reactions on how they would deal with a similar situation. This is understandable but not applicable. In the past, I rarely ever did what anyone expected me to do.

This is not about denial; it is about acceptance. Acceptance for me does not preclude change. It is more about blending realities, weaving the idea of identity. Fluctuation and adaptation are important qualities. I truly view this entire experience as adding to my life. There are some things I cannot do now, but what an opportunity to experience and learn new stuff. The way I see it, most people don't ever go through this. This experience means a lot to me. In many ways, I choose to see it as a positive over a negative. There are other things I could have experienced, but maybe I did not need to. I am not sure that I could have learned as much from anything else.

By writing this book, I have had the unique opportunity to reflect upon my life so far. To say my life has been very interesting doesn't even begin to scratch the surface. I am so glad that I can see this, although as it was happening, I didn't recognize how special it was at all. I have heard that when you are dying, you "review" your life. I feel like I am "reviewing" sans death. There are some things I would change if I could. I know there are some horrible experiences that have happened to others that I wish would vanish, for instance, racism, homophobia, rape, incest, child abuse, etc. These have absolutely impacted on my life. On the whole, I feel incredibly fortunate. My life could be very ordinary, which would be fine, but in fact it is extraordinary. If this were a work of fiction, I'm not sure I would believe it. If my life were a narrative, well, I would appear larger than life. Believe me, this is a weird kind of recognition. I am not special; however my divergences have led to some fascinating experiences and lessons. These I would not trade for anything.

I never felt slim enough or beautiful enough. What a

wake-up call, what a friggin' realization! I know these are issues that many women struggle with, but what a major lesson for me. I used to be good friends with a model. Talk about always feeling like you just do not measure up. She would never make me feel inadequate overtly, but what a standard. Not because of her, I felt fat and ugly most of the time. I still deal with feelings of inadequacy. It is a huge paradox because I was in an industry (performance) that valued looks. She was also married to a model. Getting together with them was so full of meaning. What a stunning family they were to me. Of course, they also had a "gorgeous" baby. Oy. I used to be an actor, so I did have a version of what I looked like beyond my perspective. You do not need to act in order to know what your "reflection" is. I still held on to the belief that I was less than acceptable physically.

Even though I had lovers and people were attracted to me, it was difficult to accept that I was all right. And I knew better on several levels, yet this was incredibly challenging for me. A friend once told me to avoid beauty magazines because of my issues with body image. I knew they airbrushed everything, including bodies to make them even thinner, but they were so compelling. Even if it is all ideology, it's a bugger.

On the one hand, I deal with certain body images and issues that most women have to deal with, like beauty, weight and aging. (Some men, too, of course, but that is a different book. I once wrote an article that dealt with men as sex objects entitled "I Should Have Smelled Him, Obviously"[7]

---

7 *Fab Magazine*, No. 195, August 1-14, 2002, pp. 118-120.

Now I would write about the detriment of viewing men as objects. In this age of "metrosexuality," this would be very possible. At the time, I wanted access to the "gaze." I wanted access to objectification.) Many of these issues are tied into images in magazines. I strongly believe these aspects reflect the era we live in. There is also ideology, but even this shifts with time. Could it be that the body and time are linked?

There was a barometer that I wanted access to—to how I wanted to look. It didn't matter that it was fake. I believe that is why there is a fascination with Barbie®. Many of us have heard of that woman who had several surgeries to look like her. Cindy Jackson[8] has these quotes on her Web site: "The new and improved Cindy Jackson: A bombshell who wasn't born that way... she lived a real-life Cinderella story." (Joan Rivers); "No one knows more about cosmetic surgery—from both sides of the scalpel. She's living proof of her unique expertise." (*The Times*); "A trailblazing pioneer, she did the first and original Extreme Makeover 15 years before the hit TV series. In another 15 years, they'll be doing what Cindy Jackson is doing now." (no author attributed).

I do believe an unreal standard exists. The unreachable can be incredibly alluring. A temptation to achieve the unattainable exists. Someone I know very well used to be bulimic. We can take things to the extreme. This is understandable.

I recently heard that some guy found me beautiful. I have such a hard time believing that. Some part of me knows I am fine, but some part is messed up for sure. I don't think more introspection will change that. I mean, I am aware of

8   See <http://www.cindyjackson.com>

Romy Shiller, Ph.D. • *You Never Know*

my problem, but this is a big challenge for me. There exists so much pressure in this area.

Then I have to consider that I am a disabled woman, along with all the preconceptions that go along with the term "disabled." I know in this sense that I am a bit of a warrior. I call what I am experiencing "disability drag" and, because I have a permanent shunt in my head to drain excess fluid from my brain, I call this "cyborg drag." In many ways, I embrace my "otherness."

I thought I always knew that the physical was a manifestation of our culture. That is, what we imagine we look like is predicated by social convention. (Notions of beauty and ugliness have changed drastically throughout history.) Now I have to live as a disabled woman. This is very difficult indeed. I feel like I am judged on what I look like now more than ever. I find I am even harsh with myself. Gaining a bit of weight seems more detrimental to some than being physically disabled. Shocking but true. These days, some people prefer to have partners with "meat on their bones." In old days, gaining weight was a sign of health and beauty. I was going to say that I hope people learn from this. But everyone follows their own path, right? Maybe that's the lesson. Who knows?

I have heard "if only you were as before." Heck yeah, but I am not; and if I stay this way, I still figure I have lots to offer. Sure I look different, but if that is the measure of my worth, that would suck. I do not buy into that. No matter how difficult my issues about body image are, I have a hard time believing that.

I have learned, as a result of my current situation that it's okay to ask for help. Patience and having to learn to slow down have become very important. I can't stand waiting for anything or anyone. This is definitely a lesson for me. Patience is such a big deal now. I am no longer on my own schedule. I find I have to wait a lot. This really bothers me. So does dependency. To be dependant on others for help now is so hard for me. You do what you have to, I guess. I may not like it, and I would do things differently if I could.

Health can mean so many different things to me. On the one hand, I am very healthy. I do not have high blood pressure, high cholesterol, a heart condition or diabetes. I do not eat fried or fatty foods or red meat. On the other hand, I had this brain problem that changed my life. So health, to me, is completely relative. I ride a stationary bike now, primarily for cardiovascular exercise. I listen to music at the same time. It affords me pleasure as well as a "healthy" activity. The process of getting into the seat is quite the ordeal. I also require straps for my left hand to hold the handlebar and left foot to stay on the peddle. There is exercise before the exercise. I need supervision for now, which means I am never alone when I do this.

I have become incredibly adept at blocking out what bothers me. As you can imagine, there is little privacy now. It has become necessary for me to hold onto privacy as much as possible. This can take a lot of energy, but what's the alternative? I don't think people around me realize how taxing this can be. It might seem like a small or simple thing, but it does require focus. Maybe I am more modest than I thought. If I were a nudist, for example, I imagine part of this would be easier for me. I am far from a prude, but I feel what is personal is personal. In a major way, I have had to revise and reprioritize what matters to me. I would not ordinarily think about these things, but my life is not the usual now. I now consider what I used to take for granted. Thinking about stuff is a bonus for me; however, the practical implications are always present.

Before the first surgery, I really wanted to wash my hair, but during an MRI (magnetic resonance imaging) they stuck green tabs on my skull. I didn't want them to fall off. They were beginning to slip down. I mentioned this to the doctors and anyone who would listen, but was told it didn't matter. They were going to use these tabs as markers in relation to a camera to align my head during the surgery. I felt like the Bride of Frankenstein. They were not painful, but they did prevent me from doing certain things, like washing my long hair. I took a shower the morning of the surgery, I made an effort not to wet an IV that was attached to me, and was very careful not to wet my head at all. Later on, my mother told me that she and a nurse washed and cut my hair. The first surgeon would not shave my head, but they did later on. They had to shave the left side of my skull to insert the permanent shunt in my head. I had very short hair for a while, which I do not remember.

I was also very skinny apparently. When I was in rehab, much later on, my friend Jennifer commented on this and said I was "slippery like an eel." A mysterious and beautiful woman, Jen has very long (to her waist), dark hair and is a fabulous theatre director. She created *Theatre Asylum*, an innovative endeavour, and I used to be on its Board of Directors. Jen rediscovered her Jewish heritage and introduced me to the Minsk synagogue in Kensington Market, Toronto. I have never met anyone so creative and imaginative. She is an adventurer of the heart and spirit.

Now I have an MRI of my brain every year as part of a neurology checkup. This consists of a dye-injected IV inserted into my hand for contrast purposes. I do not look forward to this, to say the least. Things could be much worse, but this is quite uncomfortable. It is a major pain in the ass. Additionally, there is always the possibility that the tumour has returned. Can you say stress? Knowledge is good, but what a way to get it.

When I became conscious, my close friend Daniel P., who is dark, extremely handsome, a brilliant human being and very spiritual—if there is such a thing as soul-love, I have it for him—brought me a beautiful orchid that lasted an uncommonly long time in the hospital. Now I notice that flowers in general last a very long time around me. Many people have observed this—I do not question it. This is kind of eerie, I suppose; it is certainly economical—I love flowers. A total stranger once gave me a flower at a shopping centre. I put it in a vase and it lasted so long one of my physiotherapists, who visits me at home, mentioned something to that effect. I just thought it was pretty. It also reminded me how very kind strangers can be. My parents' friends Sunny and Lenny, whom I love dearly, sent me gorgeous flowers in a vase with a floral design around the top. They sent me many stunning items, but I have to say I adore the vase. It is completely fantastic to me.

In the Spring of 2005 I went to the Tulip Festival in Ottawa, where I took photos for the first time since I left

Toronto. My objective, even though we were in the capital and there were the Parliament Buildings to see, was to go to this festival. I mean, wow, a whole festival devoted to flowers—my favourite kind—tulips. It was a veritable sea of tulips. Colours were grouped together. There was a host of colours. I felt like I must have gone to heaven. I found it really spectacular and I was thrilled to be there. My computer is now surrounded by pictures of tulips. Some I took, some my dad took. They might be inanimate, but they remind me of when I was there and how awesome they are.

Chapter 4

Oy!

THERE IS NO REALITY EXCEPT THE ONE CONTAINED WITHIN US.
THAT IS WHY SO MANY PEOPLE LIVE SUCH AN UNREAL LIFE. THEY
TAKE THE IMAGES OUTSIDE THEM FOR REALITY AND NEVER ALLOW
THE WORLD WITHIN TO ASSERT ITSELF.
—Herman Hesse

I'M NOT CRAZY ABOUT REALITY, BUT IT'S STILL THE ONLY PLACE
TO GET A DECENT MEAL.
—Groucho Marx

I THINK I have always been a very philosophical person. That
is, I always thought about what most people think is odd. I
have always been very open-minded. I am pretty much willing to consider anything, and I imagine this mindset helps
me now. There are so many differences I now have to face. I
feel mentally prepared for these. My inescapable obstacle is
that most people do not accept where I am now. Some people equate acceptance with giving up (the hope of recovery,
I guess), which I never do. So, unfortunately, my challenges
are more with other people than with myself. I find I often
have to be a psychologist. As I am not trained for this, and
because my focus is on physiotherapy, I find this difficult.
This I do not need. I do not resent it; I just wish people

would get it. It is the reactions of others to my current physical status that brings me down the most. I feel like I am not believed when I say I am okay. I know the marker of difference from "before" is substantial. When I say most people could not deal with this, I can look at the reactions around me and see my evidence. Attitude means so much.

I called the distant view from the window in my hospital room a medieval village, because that is what I imagined one would look like. Right across the street was a funeral home and a Chinese food restaurant. Oy!

I have always been fascinated by the nature of "reality," although I believe in consequences for our actions. And, when we break a bone, we break a bone. I guess our "soul" remains consistent. Things like identity and personality seem to be part genetic and part environmental.

I never took "reality" as a given. Maybe that is why my dreams meant so much to me. Aside from them being very telling of my state of mind at the time, they were so "real." I did not have one nightmare the entire time.

I have always believed that we are limited by our senses. We depend on them too much. We imagine we can know "truth." Curiosity is a good thing, but it's helpful to acknowledge our limitations. A fish in a fishbowl only knows what a fish in a fishbowl knows, right? I believe we are like the fish. We can only know so much because of our state of being. This does not mean we do not ask the important questions. It just means that our answers might be somewhat skewed. I guess we need to be humble.

My dreams before surgery were not as vivid as when I was in the coma, but some were very interesting. I once had a dream that *God was a copperish-coloured wave travelling through space.* I do not believe that God would have a face or gender. Or that God would be white and old. I do believe in an energy or force. Maybe I am wrong. I guess that I will eventually find out.

The earliest dream I remember from when I was a child was that *I was an older Polynesian woman holding a baby and I was struck by a tidal wave and killed.* This dream was recurring and very scary to me. I would wake up holding my breath and feel like I was suffocating. I never told anyone about it. Weird.

One of my favourite old dreams involved *me paddling in a canoe on a very calm lake surrounded by pine trees. All I could hear was the dipping of the oars in the water.* I knew this was the meaning of God.

I know that my ideas of God and religion are different from most people, and I am very comfortable with that. I am also proud to be Jewish. No matter what I believe, I would be persecuted by certain extremists. Anti-Semitic comments are freaky and stupid to me. I really like my heritage.

I have never seen 3-D because I have been blind in my left eye since birth. I always believed that I had a better understanding of life because of it. Anyway, to me, there are more dimensions than we generally believe in. I have never seen a 3-D film, mostly because those funny glasses don't work on me. But I could see well enough to drive—I sold my car primarily because I didn't want to contribute to the pollution problem. I used to ride streetcars instead.

I have heard that my vision is like a television screen. I did think that television was an accurate representation of the world—at least visually. The two dimensions and flatness are how I see everything. This might seem strange to many people, but not to me. I am used to it. My brain has compensated for the lack of visual depth. Rather than feel limited by my visual situation, I used to think I would make a really good cinematographer because of it. Isn't it amazing what we can think of?

My vision is much worse now, which is very difficult on many levels for me. It is nearly impossible to read without magnification. I truly do not believe that I will ever have the option to drive again. The vision in my right eye, the one I can see out of, bobs up and down. I cannot see properly when things are moving and I need to sit very close to a television set, even when wearing glasses. A very nice counsellor came to see me from the Montreal Association the Blind (MAB) and she set up an appointment with a low-vision specialist. I saw her again at the institute. I feel such a bond with her. It is almost indescribable. If I had a sister, I would want her to be her.

I had extensive vision testing and I have to say that not only was everyone superb at the MAB, but they were incredibly personable. I will have access to an apparatus that makes it easier to read. I tested out a machine that makes text larger. While I am so grateful that this exists, I find it unbelievable that I need to use it. I used to read so much, from novels, biographies and academic works to non-fiction special interest books and more.

When I use the computer (for email or writing, for example), I make the font very big and the contrast really helps. I now use a regular keyboard with categorically big letters stuck on, which was provided to me by the MAB. Previously, I used a mouse with a large ball on the end, like a huge joystick. I could see to hold it, but it was big and bulky. I saw a computer specialist at the MAB to check out new programs for people with compromised vision. The one I will get makes text larger and voices what I have written. It also reads my email to me. He was very helpful and I will go back there for training on how to properly use the program.

There is what I can only call a "facilitator" at the MAB. She is a low-vision specialist. She attends all my appointments with me and answers my questions as they pop up. She really adds a smoothing-out quality to every experience. I liked her from the moment I met her. She treats me with respect and kindness. I am never made to feel "less" because of my disabilities. It must be quite difficult for her to understand what I am saying, but the effort to comprehend is there. There is a very "real" quality to our interactions.

My vision impedes progress on a rehabilitation level. For instance, I am given exercises in speech therapy that are difficult to read, and if I hold the paper up to my face to see, I block the way I sound. This certainly does not help matters. My speech therapist has to read my exercises out loud for me. Homework is very tricky. In addition to everything I have to deal with, my vision is one tough reality—and very horrible to me.

It will be necessary to have surgery on my left eye. It is inverted: It stays to the right, pointing at my nose, and I have no control over it. An eye doctor said I would have more range if it were corrected. I can only move it so far when I do exercises in physiotherapy. I cover my right eye in an attempt to move it. I also imagine it will look better to have a straight eye. Procedures and surgeries are my new reality. Ouch. This surgery will be extremely complex because of my very low vision.

In a way, it is pretty bizarre that I think about reality the way I do and that this has happened to me. I do not think we are given more than we can handle. It is possible to meet what feels insurmountable. I may not like it, but I can handle this.

There are some horrible things that happen to very good people without justification. I am very curious about how they handle this and what is done with their experience. Experiences are lessons that can be opportunities for reactions. I guess one's reaction will speak volumes about who one is.

My physical reality is truly difficult. But really, who do I know that had brain surgery, went into a coma for so long and had "akinetic mutsim"? I lived through it all, although one neurosurgeon did tell my parents that I was critically ill. I think it is fascinating that I am considered a "medical mystery." While in the coma, I had bizarre dreams and lived to tell about them. I even get to analyze my whole experience. I am my own personal reality experiment.

I was always me, no matter what stage I was at. I did think differently, but still, there was a part of me that remained me. There was a "fog" for a very long time, but through it all, I was who I was. This has made me think that people who are mentally challenged are just different. Even animals are aware: The way they perceive reality might be different from how we do, but it certainly does not mean they do not think. My feeling is that whatever the initial cause, acting upon intention is more than valid and meaningful. Imagine if, like animals, we did not have language. Would this mean we were not thinking? We would think differently. If we are talking about "intelligence," well, there are gradations between humans, right? Personally, I do believe that different species can be very intelligent. It is all about perception and a willingness to expand oneself. We all have preconceptions that can be altered. Conjoined twins were born in Canada. They are very healthy, but they are joined at the head. We are used to seeing babies and people look and act a certain way. They face major challenges if they stay together, but if they do, then we would have to alter our perception. If our perception is negative, imagine the effect on them and us. I think change is about adaptation. I need to apply this philosophy to my life now.

I do believe we can change over time, but semantically we are who we are.

I really do not believe in inside and outside regarding the body. There is a physical "inside." There is a heart inside a chest-cavity and there is a brain inside a skull, for example. We add meaning to these terms. When I talk about discrepancies between my mind and body, I do not mean inside and out—I just mean there appears to be a difference. Maybe that is why I never felt trapped.

Right before my first surgery, Jennifer Lopez was engaged to Ben Affleck; when I became conscious she was about to marry Marc Anthony. No wonder I thought I was still dreaming. I am sorry to say this, but I never laughed so hard.

Before the brain surgery, I watched a lot of films on "reality," such as *Dark City* (1998, Alex Proyas), *Groundhog Day* (1993, Harold Ramis), *The Matrix* (1999, Andy Wachowski, Larry Wachowski), *Sliding Doors* (1998, Peter Howitt), in addition to many others. I also read tarot cards for myself and for other people, and consider myself pretty psychic. I am a popular culture junkie.

Chapter 5

James-Paul

Hold on to what is good, even if it's a handful of earth. Hold on to what you believe, even if it's a tree that stands by itself. Hold on to what you must do, even if it's a long way from here. Hold on to your life, even if it's easier to let go. Hold on to my hand, even if I've gone away from you. Hold on.
—A Pueblo Indian Prayer

Don't be dismayed at goodbyes. A farewell is necessary before we can meet again. And meeting again after a moment or lifetime is certain for those who are friends.
—Richard Bach

Don't mistake coincidence for fate.
—John Locke (from the television series, Lost)

I helped one of my oldest friends, Jamie, a medical doctor; die about six months before my brain surgery. "Helped" in the sense that he wanted me to be a spiritual adviser to him. He had dirty blond hair, a terrific body that he obviously worked on and a wicked grin.

I have been asked what Jamie must have seen in me to ask me to be his spiritual adviser. Aside from all of the psychic stuff, he must have seen peace and inner strength. We talked constantly and I got him a book on dying. I remember that he underlined certain passages. That some parts resonate with others is all we can hope for. To me, expectations are futile, but they do creep up.

I remember us both crying on his bed in the hospital when he was sick, because we both could not see my future. If only we had known. Jamie would have been so angry at my condition. Knowing him, he would have tried to "fix" me. I once tripped down a staircase, pulling several ligaments and fracturing my foot. He wheeled me to a hospital emergency room for an x-ray and took me to his favourite doctor.

Jamie may not know this, but the way he handled his disease—he was in his thirties and had terminal lung cancer, and he had been a non-smoker all of his life—really prepared me to deal with what happened to me. I never feared death. In fact, I heard his voice calling my name when he died.

Through him, two people would become my lawyers, Veena and Glen. I learned of the concept of caregivers, which I was unaware of. I became friends again with people I had lost touch with. And so, I became prepared in very spiritual and pragmatic ways.

Jamie once fell off his bike and damaged his teeth. He called me from the hospital. Now every time I have to hold onto a bar, I think of his experience and hold on a little tighter. What he went through, on so many levels, has affected my life.

Some of my favourite memories of Jamie include the time we drank Baby Duck, very cheap "champagne"—if you could even call it that—right before our high school graduation photo. We bought it in a yummy little sandwich shop we used to frequent as teenagers near the school. For fun, we used to play on the see-saws in a park close by. Jamie's sense of fun was contagious and invigorating. "Play" was not only spontaneous, but required. It is amazing that we both turned out to be quite studious: two doctors, one medical, one philosophical.

After high school, we were on a swim team together. If it were not for his insistence, I never would have done it. Now that I cannot swim, this is hugely significant. It is incredible to me that we did this. I remember once he was starting a backstroke and I was doing a front crawl, and by freak accident, he punched me. I have never seen anyone so apologetic or concerned. I was more anxious about him than my own self.

While at McGill University, Jamie "roasted" me for my birthday. He doctored some photos of me and stuck them on a wall. They were clever, funny and extremely flattering. I was a superstar in each photo. I still have them. He must have devoted plenty of time putting the new photos together. We took many classes together, including one on existentialism and a class named "Possible Worlds," and we performed in some of the same plays, such as *Dr. Faustus* (Marlowe) and *Macbeth* (Shakespeare). Jamie was extremely bright and creative.

We went for a brief holiday together to the Town of Magog in the Eastern Townships of Quebec. It was very last-minute; we almost did not go. We tried a sauna together that made us laugh hysterically. It was so comfortable being with him. He was like a brother to me. He used to call me his sister. We were in our early twenties.

Jamie was there to support me in our late twenties, when I discovered a friend had died in a horrific bicycle accident. We went to his apartment, where I made important phone calls. When he was diagnosed with lung cancer, he referred to Cicely. I said it was not the same. Her accident and his death might have had the same result, but that is where the commonality ends. I would not make a comparison between an accident and an illness.

Jamie and I danced together throughout the years. When we were teenagers, we went on a "club crawl," going to several nightclubs, dancing together. It was magical and there was no inhibition. Dancing was a huge part of our friendship. I remember dancing with him well into our thirties. We would often bump into each other at nightclubs and simply dance together. It was our language: our way of communicating with one another.

I would have to say Jamie was present at many crucial moments during my lifetime. He was a very special person. I am definitely very lucky to have known him. He was such a witness to whatever I was going through. It is incredible to be seen that way. Even though I feel his presence, I do miss him very much. I wonder what our forties would have brought.

I used to read a lot about death, reincarnation (if we do reincarnate, I feel we reincarnate into the past as well as the future) and quantum physics. I would make certain connections where there were none. I had a feeling that reincarnation and quantum physics were interconnected. Speaking of loss, of course, we miss the person or entity, like a beloved animal. But I have never been scared of death. I guess that I had a good mental foundation for all of this.

One of the hardest things I ever did was have my beloved black and white cat Annie put down when she was very sick. She was with me almost every day for eighteen years. Jamie was one of the kind souls who looked after Annie when I had to go out of town. After she was gone, I knew she was in a safe place, but I cried a lot. I miss her so much now. I really do not think it is a contradiction, this missing of the person or entity and knowing they are at peace. Either one can inform the other or you just separate both. To me, both coexist and are valid. For my part, I do not question this. What I have taken away from my life experience is that love crosses all boundaries.

My life has shown me that there is very little distinction between human, animal, gender, race or class. These are all fabricated set-ups that we either buy into or not. There are real ramifications for each category, but I believe we can resist classifying. What is important to remember is we have a choice. You may ask how do we become not human? Well, I have a permanent shunt in my head, so I suppose I am a cyborg (part person and part machine.) But then again, I consider people with piercings cyborgs as well.

Annie may have been a different species from me, but I never considered her my "pet." I named her after Annie Lennox, whom I met years later. I told her that I named my cat Annie after the *Touch* album because my cat, like Annie Lennox, had a mask, too. Annie Lennox drew what I call "Annie Art" for me. Essentially, it was a hand-drawn picture of a cat. It hung on my apartment wall until I went into the hospital.

It is awful to judge someone based on skin colour, heritage or financial situation. I remember I got into an argument about this with an elderly gentleman at a social gathering when I was much younger. I stood by what I thought and felt no matter who was listening or what trouble I might get into; I was willing to risk it all for what I believed to be right. I still am.

As for gender, well, I wrote my doctoral thesis on it (*A Critical Exploration of Cross-Dressing and Drag in Gender Performance and Camp in Contemporary North American Drama and Film*), so I have a lot to say. I do not believe that sex is the same as gender. We are born female or male (sex), then we dump a whole lot of meaning onto what it means to be female or male (gender). For instance, we wrap baby girls in pink blankets and baby boys in blue ones. Why? Historically, females were not supposed to work. Men were the apparent providers. This has changed over time and shows us it is far from a given. I believe we can play with gender: There are gradations to being male and female, and we can resist the codes that we are born into. I really love this subject matter and taught a university course on it. My intention was to disseminate knowledge on gender. I am aware that gender can be a very touchy subject. This did not stop me.

By coincidence, Jamie and I shared an admiration for *Buffy the Vampire Slayer*, the supernatural series on television. Jamie had a poster of Sarah Michelle Gellar playing Buffy on his wall. We both had the CD of the musical version of one of the episodes. I really like strong female protagonists.

Jamie was cremated; his ashes were divided between eighteen of his friends. They were lovingly wrapped in red cloth. I put his ashes in a Buffy tin—it is his urn for now.

Chapter 6

Mush

ALL THAT WE SEE OR SEEM, IS BUT A DREAM WITHIN A DREAM.
—Edgar Allan Poe

OUR TRUEST LIFE IS WHEN WE ARE IN DREAMS AWAKE.
—Henry David Thoreau

IN DREAMS BEGINS RESPONSIBILITY.
—William Butler Yeats

IN ANOTHER DREAM, *I was in a different room but still in a hospital, one that was on the beach. I was in a high-rise that had takeout.* I must have been hungry.

In reality, from August 2003 through July 2004, I had a feeding tube that connected directly to my stomach. I started eating what I call "mush" at the hospital in March. What seems to surprise people is that my feeding tube remained in place for an extra six months, even after I had come out of the coma. In the beginning, I mostly ate applesauce. They left the tube in during the initial test period to make certain I was hydrated and as a precautionary measure. When I did start to eat and drink even with the tube in place, the liquids were thickened with a bulking substance and the solids were made very soft—like a puree. Yum, eh? It was gross but necessary. I was allowed to put a popular sauce on everything just to give it flavour.

There are still some things I will not eat, just to be on the safe side, like popcorn, nuts and chips. Actually, I find it difficult to swallow these things, so I avoid them. I will not chew gum or suck on mints. Popcorn is the most difficult. I am worried that a part will lodge in my throat and I will not be able to swallow it down. It feels very dangerous to me. So I just do not eat it at all. When I go to movie theatres and people around me are eating popcorn, I long for it. Weird, but I never really liked popcorn until I could not have it.

One of my earliest jobs was working at the concession stand at a movie theatre. I used to sell popcorn to patrons. I remember serving Pierre Elliot Trudeau[9], former Prime Minister of Canada, and his sons Sacha and Michel. This was such a high point for me. I once had a part in a movie where I was called the "Popcorn Girl." So, in many ways, this food item was a backdrop to my life. It represents more than food to me. The concept "popcorn" is a part of my past life. It is a symbol, for sure. No wonder I miss it now.

I imagined for the longest time I had a plastic box inside my stomach that was connected to the feeding tube. Ridiculous, but it made perfect sense at the time. Now it is just funny.

My feeding tube occasionally got blocked, so I hear. Believe it or not, they used cola to unblock it. I swear. "They" are the nurses and my mother.

---

9 See < http://simple.wikipedia.org/wiki/Pierre_Trudeau>

My parents flew to Toronto from Europe from almost the moment I heard that I had a tumour in my brain. I went to the emergency room after feeling so sick. It is lucky that I inadvertently walked into a hospital with a reputation for a well-known neurological unit. At first, the officials at the hospital thought I had meningitis and I was isolated. After the CT scan, a doctor came into the room and said I might have cancer—I did not. What a shock when the results of that first scan were revealed.

In the emergency room waiting area, I had to sit alone. Then I was escorted to a room where I was isolated so I could not infect anyone. I remember thinking that if I had meningitis, I might need a lumbar puncture and that this could hurt. I watch so much television, including medical shows, so I am sure I was influenced by a bit of melodrama. My entire experience felt like reality TV. They did a CT scan simply to rule out any genetic or inherited factors. That is when they discovered the tumour in my brain. Luckily they found it, but what a surprise, to say the least—very dramatic to be sure.

That night, a close friend, Larissa, was with me when I was placed in the intensive care unit for the night. She is a very special and unique person whom I love enormously. I remember her taking away my sneakers. She eventually gave them to my parents. A really caring nurse looked after me that night.

Apparently I spent six weeks (following my surgeries) in the intensive care unit and the neurological step-down unit, which is intensive care for brain trauma. A neurosurgeon visited me the morning after my first surgery and members of my family said I was able to lift the correct hands upon command. I do not remember this. It truly seemed like I was improving. I had some auditory memory the first day. I remember my bother Doug telling me at some point that there had been a huge blackout along the Eastern seaboard, but that I would be okay. I remember that very well and clearly. I thought about what impact the blackout would have on me.

My mom gave me her impressions of the blackout later on. Not only was the blackout inconvenient, but she had a daughter in major recovery in a hospital. Thank goodness the hospital had backup power. It was my mom's birthday the day after my first surgery, which occurred on August 13, and that evening (August 14) was the blackout. She is grateful she and my bothers had cell phones so that they could communicate with one another. The hospital would not let any of my family visit me that night. It must have been very frightening for them.

In another dream, *I was in a hospital ward with other people situated next to rushing water, like a thin canal. The water was very dark. There was a large city in the distance. The ward was like a big country cabin, but with hospital beds and a hard floor. Windows existed, which let in the light from outside and through which I could see the water and city. There was sand just outside.*

Larissa went to Japan to teach children English and other subjects. She had made plans to do this months before. I had gone shopping with her to get appropriate clothing. It was fun but sad. We found good stuff, but the knowledge she would be leaving was difficult. She looks like a pixie to me. I always considered her an angel, without all of the frilly accoutrements we imagine goes with this word (angel). She definitely looks more hard-core than that. Larissa has blond, sometimes dark, spiky short hair. She is tiny and has a laugh that melts your heart. Larissa is brave, creative, fluid and very kind. She is so much smarter than she knows. Larissa is light in human form. Her entire class in Japan sent me homemade get-well cards that were astonishing, which my mom put up on my hospital room wall. I remember them so well from when I came out of the coma. I adored them. It was amazing to me that her whole class, who had no idea who I was, made cards for me. What an honour.

Initially, it was not so easy to see my parents. Especially my father: Until this time, we did not get along. But I heard that he spent many hours in the library researching all aspects of my illness, especially my coma. I had sleep-wake cycles, but actually all I remember are my dreams.

I knew that telling my parents the news would be majorly disruptive and devastating—they had megaplans. My mom was going to lead a university-based tour to Russia—but I figured they needed, and would want, to know. I never questioned this. I called my brother Doug from the hospital emergency room and he called them for me. They were staying with their friends Sunny and Lenny in the south of France. Lenny woke them up and told them they had an urgent call from my brother. Sunny arranged transportation to the airport and asked to be kept informed. She called my parents very often and made many worthwhile suggestions. It was a big ordeal for my parents to get back to Canada on such short notice. I had faith in their love for me, and it was truly comforting that they were there. I felt their strength and knew they would be on my side and fight for me if they had to.

My parents ended up being quite unique and creative. I am more than glad they did not care what hospital staff thought. I am sure they faced huge amounts of opposition. I have heard that they were quite a presence, much more involved than most parents usually are. This must have bothered some professionals; I would not have expected anything less of them. I know my situation was all-consuming, but they made an effort to retain a semblance of their own life. I am sure that much of their conversation revolved around me, but at least they had each other to "escape" into.

In another bizarre dream, *I was married to a top chef and recipes were made of hot chocolate on my back. The in-laws loved me.*

I feel so lucky, which is freaky, considering I'm in a wheelchair, my voice and speech are wonky, the left side of my face does not move and my whole left side is much weaker than my right. My left eye appears bigger than my right one. The vision in my right eye bobs up and down. My right hand is locked in a piano-player-like position. I cannot raise my left arm beyond a certain point and my left hand is pretty ineffective. I guess that I am lucky to be alive. I mean, I prepared for the eventuality of my own demise on the operating table, but I guess that it did not hit me until now.

I know that this will not make many people happy and that it is probably not politically correct, but here goes anyhow. I did not feel the feeding tube. I would have kept it in if I needed it to live. Now I feel that if I needed a respirator to live, if I didn't feel any pain on it and if the people who loved me wanted to take care of me, fine with me. Before the surgery, I thought that tubes would be such a hassle, now I know that for me they are not.

I had a dream that *they wanted to take out a tube, so I was moved to a forest. There, a female doctor with short dark hair looked after me.* That is all I remember about that dream.

Following the initial surgery, I was on a respirator for eleven days and they prepared for a tracheotomy, but finally I did not need either. They never did the trach, and I was taken off the respirator. My friends could not visit during this time, so they wrote me letters, which my mom apparently read to me. My clever friend Minda, who is often compared to Michelle Pfeiffer, was concerned about writing about daily life when I was experiencing something so major. I think that daily life is probably just what I needed to hear about. The ordinary or everyday must have seemed like quite the luxury. The difference is substantial but comforting. Minda is a tremendously talented costume designer who works in theatre and film. She has a wondrous curiosity that propels her towards the uncommon. I had a feeling I would know her the first time I ever saw her. Now, Minda is one of my closest friends.

I heard about Terri Schiavo[10] when they were removing her feeding tube. She is always on my mind now.

---

10 See <http://en.wikipedia.org/wiki/Terri_Schiavo>

Chapter 7

What a Concept

MY ABSOLUTE OLDEST and dearest friend in the world, Joy
(we have known each other for at least thirty years), came often all the way from Montreal to see me in the hospital. She
is family to me, and it still means a great deal to me that she
was there. She was very close to Jamie as well and was utterly
devastated when he died. It is unimaginable to me that she
had to go through my "illness" as well. To me, she looks like
a combination of Annie Lennox and Ellen DeGeneres. She
is a chartered accountant and has a wicked sense of humour.
Joy constantly makes me laugh. Her candour is extremely
appreciated. I can always count on her to tell it like it is.
There is much about her that I find value in. I will always
love Joy unconditionally.

Warren, my eldest brother, lives quite far away but came

to see me as much as he could. I love him so much and it meant the world to me when he was there. If I were a casting director in a major Hollywood studio, he would be Keanu Reeves. Not that they look similar: Warren has curly brown hair. I would never take Warren's visits for granted. He is so funny, handsome, smart, creative, kind and giving. He has given my life meaning. To me, he inspires confidence and trust. I am exceedingly fortunate to know him. I always felt he was a spiritual soulmate. He is in business and, at the same time, he is extremely creative. His writing blows me away and his thought-provoking ideas are remarkable. He is incredibly wise. I never tire of listening to him. He is truly inspirational to me.

Doug, my younger brother, with curly light brown hair and piercing blue eyes, who is conscientious to a fault, came to visit me every weekend. I'm not sure if he realizes this, but he has a very creative spirit. He has a Ph.D. in the research side of cognitive psychology, but I think it is awesome to hear him play guitar. He is amazingly talented. I framed one of his paintings because I liked it immensely and because it was exceptional. He made it in grade three. Doug did not live in the same city where I was hospitalized, but he lived closer than Warren and Joy. Tons of responsibility fell on him. He and my sister-in-law, Sonya, cleared out my apartment and put all my stuff in storage. They also found a new home for Leiloo, my caramel and white eight-year-old cat.

Initially, my family put Leiloo in what I call a "cat-spa." Essentially, it was a fancy-shmancy boarding facility for animals. I am grateful she was there while I was in the hospital. She was taken care of extremely well. I feel incredibly responsible for her well-being so I continue to be relieved for that.

We were at the tail end of the SARS[11] crisis in Toronto, and many of my friends had a difficult time gaining access to the hospital to see me before my operation. However, they were incredibly persistent.

Several days before my first surgery, I took photos outside of the hospital with some of my closest friends: Larissa, Minda, Daniel P. and Jennifer. They were able to be present on short notice. I still have and cherish that photo.

In late December or January, I don't know which—I started to dream about Linda. She was a private physiotherapist hired by my mother to fill in on the days that were not scheduled by my regular hospital physiotherapists. I dreamt the following: *that the whole session was over*. I mean, I went through the entire session not knowing if it was a dream or reality. What a concept. I was really relieved when it was over. Now that I think of it, it was so *The Matrix* of me. I lived a dream world. I still don't know if it was a dream or real. I find this pretty stunning.

In the real world, after I came out of the coma, I do remember Linda trying to sit and stand with me. She would also, what she called, "unwind my eyeballs," which just involved her lightly touching my eyelids. It was so relaxing. She used a Myofascial[12] technique on me. She was involved again in my rehab during the summer of 2004. Linda became a friend of mine.

---

11 See <http://www.cdc.gov/NCIDOD/SARS>
12 See <http://en.wikipedia.org/wiki/Myofascial_Release>

Strangely enough, I do not remember the first time I ever met her, but it was never sudden, shocking or surprising to me that she was a new part of my life. What I gather from this is that some part of me was aware that she was there, although I was still in a coma. Some part of me must have known she was on my side. This happened with several other people as well. It all really blows me away. I find it truly interesting, if not validating, too. To me, it really underscores my belief system. I believe that when we are out of it, we are still aware of certain things.

I remember dreaming that *one of my friends was two different people, like identical twins. They both shared the same husband, but had different personalities.* I remember thinking in my dream, "This is weird."

Happiness means different things depending on what you are talking about. Happiness can really run the gamut. It can be esoteric, like love, friendship, good conversation and good sex, or certain things, like some beautiful dishes, tastes, colours, smells or jewellery that makes you happy. Obviously, surviving my ordeal makes me happy, but all of these things are hardly equivalent. These days, I believe I am considered a happy person. I wonder if it has more to do with how my response to my new situation is being perceived by others than any real change on my part.

Happiness was a topic on the radio the other day. The callers all articulated a difference amongst each other and the various things that made them happy. It got me thinking about the idea of happiness and my generally positive response to the life I am living. Mostly it is about coping now, but certain things do make me happy. I am glad for that.

Maybe I am just more aware of the possibilities for happiness than I used to be. That is not to say everything is dandy. It is not, but I do, to use an old cliché, see light at the end of the tunnel. Not only that, but I find "the light" in the here and now. There is a lot of stuff that tickles my fancy, and I let it do just that. Then again, I always did. Even in my doctoral thesis, a serious undertaking, I wrote about camp; it can be a very funny subject. I was entertained for sure.

Needless to say, certain comedy does make me happy. I laugh a lot now. Then again, I have very funny people around me. I even laugh at myself. For instance, I do the crossword every day with my dad. Once he gave me a clue that was "Delhi-wear," I thought he meant deli-wear. I wondered what does one wear in a deli? An apron? This mistake on my part still kills me. I mean, really, who thinks that?

My brother Warren and I have a tradition of sending each other calendars for the New Year. In 2006, he sent me what I suppose is an earnest calendar full of pictures of tractors. I looked forward to the tractor of the month and I found the whole thing hysterical.

I would not characterize myself as "happy," but I do think I am positive. I truly believe things could be much worse. I know my current situation is quite dire to many people, and I have left quite a bit behind, but the alternative is harsher. I am here, and no matter how yucky it gets, this is so much better to me than nothing. I do not believe in "nothing" anyways. I really feel that there is something "else." Despite all of the challenges, I really do try to accept where I am. At times, I feel that others have a harder time with this than I do.

Considering it all, I am more than okay now. I choose to see what is positive over the negative. It is not that I do not recognize the negativity, but my focus lies elsewhere. I believe that "energy goes where attention flows" from or goes to. My attention is definitely on the benefits of my situation. Even when I am far from thrilled about something I experience, I ask myself to ponder over what it can bring to me. I think there are lessons in everything. Either we are open to receiving these lessons or not. Situations that we find ourselves in can offer opportunities for personal expansion. Believe it or not, what seems too hard to do is not impossible. I used to call myself a cheerleader because I would always root for people to succeed. I guess that is what I am doing now. Oy.

You know, I think that people imagine I should be more distraught about my situation than I am. That would be more "normal" (a word that I never bought into anyhow) to them.

I imagine many people have ideas of what "normal" is. Simply put, this term doesn't concern me. To me, there are many people and situations that don't fit into the so-called norm. I know I don't on many levels. For instance, I was in a situation the other day where I loudly expressed an opinion that might be contrary to those in hearing distance. I was told to keep it down by a person sitting next to me. They might be implicated by their proximity, so I did, but frankly I couldn't care less who was listening. Being contrary or dissenting is a comfort zone to me. Any perceived disapproval is completely wasted on me.

To be honest, I don't think I could be any other way. I like my attitude, I don't care one iota if this seems kooky to others. If it is chemical or otherwise, it doesn't matter to me. I always lived my life on the fringe and I guess I will continue to do so. I have always been very strong in the face of adversity. My current situation is far from the first time I have had to deal with adversity or hardship. I am not devastated or distraught about my current physicality. In so many ways, I feel prepared for this. It isn't easy but the attitude I have helps me. That is a good thing indeed. I mean, if I were angry or bitter all of the time that would certainly be a kind of hell. As it stands, I may not like what happened to me, but I had no choice in the matter. I do have a choice in what I do with myself now. There are obvious limitations, but I choose to make the most out of what I have left. Maybe I could do more in terms of a personal relationship, but I really believe that is my demon to deal with, my path, one of my lessons. I would never blame anyone for my lack of initiative. If I do not go far enough, only I am responsible. This may apply to many things, from rehab to my relationships with family and friends. I may presume that people know I am capable of only so much, but these are presumptions and could be wrong on my part.

While in the hospital, in an effort to prevent my blood from clotting, I was given injections of Heparin[13] into my lower stomach twice a day. This was as far from "happy" as you can get. I am not a person who is okay with needles: Even though they did not hurt me, it was uncomfortable. I was black and blue at the various injection sites. I felt like a

---

13 See <http://www.rxlist.com/cgi/generic/heparin.htm.>

pincushion. The injections must have started when I went into the coma and lasted until I went into rehab, about eight months later. That experience is one I cannot imagine ever forgetting. It was dramatic and constant. If you think getting an IV is an ordeal, imagine this on top of it. Holy cow!

Chapter 8

The Wormhole

MANY PERSONS HAVE A WRONG IDEA OF WHAT CONSTITUTES TRUE
HAPPINESS. IT IS NOT ATTAINED THROUGH SELF-GRATIFICATION
BUT THROUGH FIDELITY TO A WORTHY PURPOSE.
—Helen Keller

THE OPPOSITE OF LOVE IS NOT HATE, IT'S INDIFFERENCE.
THE OPPOSITE OF ART IS NOT UGLINESS, IT'S INDIFFERENCE.
THE OPPOSITE OF FAITH IS NOT HERESY, IT'S INDIFFERENCE.
AND THE OPPOSITE OF LIFE IS NOT DEATH, IT'S INDIFFERENCE.
—Elie Wiesel (October 1986)

MY GRANDFATHER EZRA died on January 10, 2004. I loved
him very much. He was in a home for seniors, and knew
nothing of what I went through. This was a blessing in many
ways. I think he would have been quite distraught about me.
He was a few days away from his 98th birthday. Just after he
passed away I started to come out of my coma. I never woke
up suddenly. It was a gradual process. I do not remember if,
or ever felt like, I left my body, although you would be hard-
pressed to find someone more open-minded and willing to
experience something out of the ordinary. Even though that
was not my experience, my belief that it does happen to others is unshaken. There did appear to be continuity for me.

It is very odd to me now, and unlike anything I have ever seen on television or film. I recently watched a film about a young woman in a coma. I thought they got it wrong. There really was no reference point for me. I imagine it must have been very difficult for those around me. My impression is that no one knew what to expect. If I did "come out the coma," would I be cognitively aware? Would I live or die? Would I need to be in a nursing home forever? My physicality might be problematic now, but at least cognitively, I am as I was.

Three days before my grandfather died, someone who knew him had a dream that he was in a car driven by my deceased grandmother. Apparently I tried to get into the rear door, but my grandpa fiercely resisted my entry. To her, this was a sign that I would be fine. How cool is that?

My maternal grandparents survived the Holocaust[14] by fleeing to Russia, but their immediate families were murdered in the Warsaw Ghetto. My mother was born while they fled, and she slept in a suitcase as a baby. I grew up hearing the tales of that war from my Baba (grandmother), who passed away several years before my first surgery. I gave the eulogy at her funeral. I remember she taught me my first song; it was "Somewhere over the Rainbow" and we watched *The Wizard of Oz* (1939, Victor Fleming) together. She was an exceptional opera singer, and it was her voice that saved those around her from being killed during the war. My grandfather, who was a pharmacist by profession, acted as her manager during her concerts. I consider them

---

14 See <http://en.wikipedia.org/wiki/The_Holocaust>

all very strong people. What an ordeal. They were certainly survivors.

I now have my Baba's Passover china, which I use every Friday evening for Shabbat. I adore this china: It evokes very pleasant memories. I'm not a religious Jew by any stretch of the imagination. I do have Shabbat, though, which is for most Jews the holiest night of the week. To me, there is a pleasing and comforting tradition in Shabbat. Like most people, I would have argumentative discussions with my family around the dinner table and at Pesach. So, my memories are not utopian, but many are associated with these dishes. My memories include the fact that I did not have my present condition. With my Baba and Grandpa gone now, the dishes mean the world to me.

I now light the Shabbat candles every Friday evening. I do that to honour my Baba—because she used to do it— and because I am a fan of ritual. Lighting the candles is like meditation to me. I get to quiet my mind and simply focus. There is something magical about lighting candles. Saying a prayer over the candles is incredibly evocative: It feels like a meditative spell has been cast. The twinkling of the candlelight and the Hebrew words are, in a word, poetic.

I get to practice my Hebrew, which is cool to me. I learned it in grade school. I went to a private Hebrew school, United Talmud Torahs of Montreal. I took Hebrew again in CEGEP (which in Quebec precedes university, if one chooses to go). I went to Vanier College for CEGEP; Joy and Jamie were there with me. I enjoy reading the prayers because they are in Hebrew, and it still boggles my mind that I know the letters. I am so grateful to do this and that I learned this language.

I know all of the prayers from Hebrew school. I like saying them, although I disagree with many of the tenets. My mother says I sound better in other languages. I asked my speech therapist about this and she thinks that it could be how the letters are aligned. That is, what follows affects how you say the words. Apparently Hebrew is that different from English.

I remember very clearly my birthday on January 12, 2004. Many friends came to see me in the hospital. I was not talking at the time (it would be a few more months), but it did not seem to matter to anyone. I was given beautiful costume jewellery that included a sparkling tiara and wand. Both occupy a prominent place in my current bedroom. I feel magical and like a princess looking at them. They are dazzling, pretty and striking.

After my birthday, I started communicating with a letter board, but I was not always successful. My hands shook a lot. I remember "saying" that I didn't like the "tilt table" used during physio with Linda. In my mind, it was literally a big Ouija board. I also spelled out that the shoes on my feet needed to come off. I really did not like shoes at the time. My feet were very sensitive and they hurt.

I was evaluated for an adapted computer by an occupational therapist named Pearl in an effort to find an access point through which I could communicate with people. First, we tried to use my eyes; then I tried to blow into a tube. Blowing air out of my mouth is very difficult for me because I cannot make a seal on the left side. I practice this in physiotherapy, occupational therapy and speech therapy. Pearl's team wanted to find a point of contact. I saw Stephen Hawking a couple of years back give a lecture on one of those computers, so I figured I was in excellent company. I swear I really thought that. Eventually, I became more responsive and no longer needed that adaptive device.

Pearl recommended a neuro massage therapist. What I remember most is that Alois shook my arms and legs quite a bit in an effort to stimulate them. Something was mentioned about using electric muscular stimulation (EMS)—which I feared, did not want and never had. I tried to spell out my concern on the letter board to my brother Doug and Sonya. They had no idea what I was "talking" about. I was very worried about this for a long time. It absolutely negatively impacted my time with Alois. I was always on the lookout. Imagine thinking you were going to be hurt by someone who is supposed to make you feel better. Probably the EMS is not painful, but in my mind at the time, I believed it would be. I could not articulate my apprehension and am sad to say that this was probably one of the worst experiences I ever had. I have never felt such fear.

A computer was very important to me. Initially, I had an adapted keyboard with some overlays that were connected to the screen. The keyboard had very big letters so I could see them and hit them with my fingers. I also had a plastic cover with holes cut out so I could use my thumb to type. The overlays gave me instant access to the Internet, which was fantastic.

In the summer of 2004, Pearl evaluated me for a new wheelchair. I will never forget that she mentioned the wheels were important because they were my legs. Also, I remember her calling me a "medical mystery," which I had not heard in relation to me, until she said it. Both comments still have a profound effect on me.

While in rehab in Toronto, after the surgeries and subsequent coma, I had several role models who are very intelligent but physically challenged. Jean Chrétien[15], a former Prime Minister of Canada, obviously had some facial paralysis and Lucien Bouchard[16], a former Premier of Quebec, lost a leg to a flesh-eating disease (necrotizing fasciitis). It was not about agreeing or disagreeing with their politics, it was about their disability and high profile. Unfortunately, I had no physically challenged female role models.

I started to squeeze in February, which was pretty major to everyone. I remember thinking about it before I actually squeezed my mom's hand. She told my dad, who did not believe I was capable of that action. He thought it was wishful thinking on her part. Imagine his surprise when I kept doing it. My sister-in-law's dad made a bell for me to squeeze in order to alert people if I needed them. My mom gave me a doll that said "I Love You" every time I squeezed it. It was around Valentine's Day, so you can just imagine.

When I became more conscious, I recall my mother wheeling me around in a wheelchair on my hospital floor pretending it was the deck of a cruise ship. We were always in a different port. This was thrilling to me. I hung onto her every word and imagined what it would be like being there.

15 See <http://en.wikipedia.org/wiki/Jean_Chr%C3%A9tien>
16 See <http://en.wikipedia.org/wiki/Lucien_Bouchard>

My dad used to wheel me around the corridors to look at some of the art on the hospital walls. He narrated each painting. I really remember one in particular that he liked the best. The colours and images really stayed with me. I looked forward to these visits immensely.

There was a very long ramp we used to take that connected buildings indoors. It felt like a flight in a spaceship to me. My family called it "The Wormhole." To Warren, it reminded him of the starship *Enterprise*.[17] It used to bring us to a very quiet part of the hospital that I really enjoyed. There were loads of offices and an area there where we used to sit and relax.

This area is where I said my first word.

I remember spending time on a different floor in the hospital that overlooked the atrium and food court. That is where I first squeezed my mom's hand. We used to go there quite a bit. I still had a feeding tube, but really didn't mind the sights and smells of the food at all. I did want pizza; I felt that I would have some eventually. When we went back for a medical check-up the next year that is what I had in the food court. It was great.

While I was in the coma, my mom would not eat, or let anyone else eat, around me. Wow. How amazing! I don't know if I would have been affected by people bringing food around; I never found out. She would not let anyone make negative comments around me. Some of the medical staff thought I would not make it and they would tell my mom to be prepared for the worst. That was not an option for her,

---

17 See <http://www.startrek.com/startrek/view/index.html>

and she did not want it to be one for me. I totally respect that. She also stuck messages on the wall behind my bed for the nurses coming on duty. For instance, I slept with my glasses on because it was hard for me to see without them and I could not reach for them. So she put up a note to insist they leave them on me at all times. Also, none of which I remember, she advised the doctors making their rounds to include me in their discussions as if I were not in a coma. Apparently she would "prep" those visiting me to include me in their conversations.

My mom tells me she did visualizations with me. She would imagine we were at a ballet studio doing exercises at a ballet barre—we would go through all of the ballet positions. She would tell me I was lifting my leg onto the barre. She also visualized that there was a ball of healing, coloured light hanging over my head. Apparently I would open my eyes once the visualization was over.

My mom also left a notebook next to my bed filled with sensory stimulation exercises for my caregivers to do with me. What dedication, eh?

I feel very lucky that she did all of those things and more. I am certain that this was an ordeal for everybody. The level of commitment is impressive. To be very honest, I am stunned. It all really resonates with me.

Chapter 9

Blank

I EXPECT NOTHING. I FEAR NO ONE. I AM FREE.
—Nikos Kazantzakis

IN THE COMA, there was nothing but dreams.

Chapter 10

Something Funny This Way Comes

THE BEAUTY OF THE WORLD HAS TWO EDGES, ONE OF LAUGHTER,
ONE OF ANGUISH, CUTTING THE HEART ASUNDER.
—Virginia Woolf

ARGUE FOR YOUR LIMITATIONS, AND SURE ENOUGH, THEY'RE
YOURS.
—Richard Bach

WHEN I CAME out of the coma, I remember that I listened to and watched comedy tapes/DVDs by Jerry Seinfeld and Ellen DeGeneres, whom I adore. This became a huge part of my life in the hospital. I hear that laughter is the best medicine, so who knows? My mom started playing these recordings while I was still in the coma. She tells me that she and Warren believed I was somewhat conscious because I would laugh at all the appropriate places. I have no memory of any of this, but it does make one think.

After the coma, I even continued having a crush on a male nurse who looked after me in the hospital and whom I had met before my first brain surgery (I say "male" nurse fairly self-consciously, because most people presume that nurses are female. That would be something else altogether, eh?) I do believe he was a part of my continuity. What do they call it when those astronauts in sci-fi travel for many years unaware of everything? Oh yeah, they're in "suspended animation." I was like that. For me, no time had passed, but it obviously had. People had their own lives to lead. It certainly was not always about me. He brought me tulips on Valentine's Day. He was so sweet and always very kind and generous to me, my family and my friends. Again, I was so lucky to have him in my life at the time. It would be such a soap opera to say we had a torrid love affair; we did not. There was an innocent quality between us. There was no steamy sex on the bathroom floor. Sorry. He visited me in rehab, but then I changed rooms and never saw him again. End of story.

My friend Minda says she was with me often when I was in the coma. Like everybody else, she was worried that I was aware but could not do anything about it. She calls it "the horror." Apparently, this is quite the syndrome. Some people feel "locked in."[18] Minda is quite glad now that I have no memory of this period of time. I wish that I could remember her being there, but like she says, it's "just as well."

In January 2004, in a very long and detailed dream, I dreamt that *I was sick and I was friends with Seinfeld. His wife asked a doctor to see me in their house. We started out driving in the country, then we went to a city.* I remember it like yesterday. I even recall what the doctor looked like.

After the coma, I was moved to another room for sleeping, which was very precarious for me. I could hear my own

18 See <http://en.wikipedia.org/wiki/Locked-In_syndrome>

breath, and it kept me awake. I would hallucinate during the day. (I saw a person sitting on my bed.) I was really made worse because of it. Besides not liking it, I could not articulate my anxiety. The whole experience totally sucked. It only lasted for a short period of time, thank goodness. Afterwards, I remained in the room I was used to.

In March, I moved out of the hospital and into a Toronto rehab centre, where I spent three months. Tracy, my physiotherapist, was truly excellent. She would visit me in the evenings and use an ultrasound machine on my left foot in an attempt to make it better. I will never forget her. During the day, I practiced throwing beanbags and trying to stand, in addition to tons of other physio stuff. Tracy had so much energy, and her positivism was infectious.

Philip was my occupational therapist. He moulded braces for my hands and taught me to propel my wheelchair. I resisted his efforts, but I was always encouraged. At one point, we looked into a mirror together. That was very problematic for me, and we stopped. I think that was the point at which I realized I had issues with mirrors.

Steve was my speech therapist; in addition to voice exercises, we sang songs by Coldplay. I love that band and own their CDs, which helped. Steve wrote out the lyrics to one of the songs ("The Scientist") for me. I thought it was cool of him then to want me to sing, and I still do. My experience with Steve was amazing and extremely beneficial. I felt like he "got me" even "after."

Before the surgeries, I could really sing. I studied voice at the Royal Conservatory of Music while I was doing my Master's and Ph.D. at the University of Toronto, and before that, with a private singing coach in Montreal from the age of thirteen until I was twenty-one. I wrote my own songs, appeared in a music video—I did an improvisation in an old insane asylum, which was taped vocally and visually—and even had a band. I was called back for a lead role in the musical *Mamma Mia*. (I was told I did not look old enough to play a mother or young enough for the daughter. Oy. Show biz…) I really could not stand the way I sounded when singing or speaking after the coma—so not like me. Singing as a part of speech therapy was a plus, for sure.

My voice may sound odd now and my speech requires loads of therapy, but I get to "say" stuff in this book that I never would have said before. In this respect, I have a new "voice." I may have lost the way I talked and sounded, but I have gained something else. I have acquired a new sense of communication. Even if one person resonates with what I have to "say," I consider myself pretty blessed.

You know, in my mind, I think as fast as I did before and I sound the same. It is discrepant now when I open my mouth to speak or sing. There is definitely a gap between what I think to say and what I say just to be understood. For instance, I still condense sentences. My current speech pathologist says I have developed strategies. I certainly have. These make it easier on everyone—including myself. My speech pathologist has also given me other strategies. The strategies I use include slowing down, over-articulating, repetition, spelling out words and even changing words. At times, I will even change languages. It's a very good thing that I now live in a bilingual province. I will often speak French, which I love.

Thank goodness I still have my vocal range. My speech pathologist has to cover her ears at times when we are doing pitch work because I go so high. I have to admit I like this. It is very validating to me. She calls it my "opera voice." I remember when I was studying voice at the Royal Conservatory; people would stand outside the door of the room I was in just to see how high I would go. I thought this was incredibly flattering. Now I am thrilled to go high at all. I saw a laryngologist who looked at my vocal chords with a special camera. She said that in addition to the neurology, I have a spasm on my vocal chords and a chemical burn due to acid reflux. I feel lucky to have a voice at all at this rate.

The difference in my singing voice is quite substantial now. Remember, I did not just sing in the shower. It is very hard to keep a simple tune. What a leap! At the Royal Conservatory, I studied and sang Italian opera, so this has been quite major. Envisage going from a truly excellent voice to a truly horrible one. I will not sing to my nephew—not only am I self-conscious, but I am terrified of scaring him. I think singing to children is incredibly special, so it's difficult for me not to do this with my very sweet nephew. Singing is a huge part of my life. If I try to sing along to a favourite tune, wow, does it sound worse than bad! So, in addition to voice and speech being affected, there has been a huge change in my singing voice. Tamara, my speech pathologist, calls this my "new normal."

After not being able to speak for seven months, the first word I said was "no" (it figures). My dad asked me if I could say "no," and to everyone's great surprise, I did. I thought about speaking out loud for days before that, so I guess a part of me knew I could not speak. We were in that very quiet area. I never tried to speak before that moment. In my dreams, I could speak. I always thought it was my choice not to speak. Now I know better. I simply could not. I never questioned why I was not talking. This might sound bizarre to you now, but for me, it was perfectly contextual. I still hardly use my voice, to sing, for example. Some things never change.

I think that part of the reason I survived is that I was not conflicted—ever. I never gave up my power. I believe that was very important. Also, I rationalized everything. Additionally, I had extremely supportive family and friends. In my mind, I did talk from the moment I was conscious onward. I had a very prominent internal dialogue. I really always considered myself speaking. I never felt "locked in" as some people thought that I may have been. They worried I was trapped "inside" my body. I never felt that way—what a *Twilight Zone* episode that would have been.

For longest time, I shortened my sentences just to be understood. This meant that I often said the bottom line, without people being privy to how I got there. To many, it appeared as if I was saying stuff out of the blue when a good deal of mental processing had gone into it. Although I still condense my sentences, I think it is very different than before. In any case, I am working on it in speech therapy. What I worry about now is people's preconceptions regarding how I sound. Over this, I really have no control.

I am going to start therapy with another voice specialist in addition to the one I now have. A lot of my vocal action is involuntary, and as such, she can only do so much. My hope is that we will stabilize my pitch so that I sound more even. Right now, there are obvious breaks in my voice, and when I speak, I tend to go too high. She has access to software that shows me my pitch: In addition to hearing my voice, I get to see it.

The very worst for me is when my mother does not understand me. I think I expect her to always get it because she is my mom. I am keenly aware that this is unreasonable, but I still feel it.

I have had several paid caregivers or attendants. It is so bizarre to know you are somebody's job. I know I am very lucky to have them, yet it feels quite odd. I personally have had so many jobs that it is not hard for me to put myself in their place. On the one hand, I am incredibly dependent on them; on the other, I have an amazing amount of power. What a strange situation to be in.

My mom now calls my caregivers "assistants," which takes them out of the realm of health care professionals. It also no longer makes me a sick person. I still require assistance, but not in the same way. I don't know that I buy into this term. I have yet to call one of my caregivers an "assistant," but I do like the impulse. Maybe the term "caregiver" justifies my current situation. Who knows? Needing help is so different than wanting help. If I think about celebrities with assistants, I imagine they are fortunate because they probably have a choice. I really don't have a choice; I require assistance. Obviously, it would be so different if I didn't need help. This is one of my hardest lessons. Even if I don't like the person or situation, I go on, because I have to. It's not always easy or pleasant, but the way I see it, these are the cards I have been dealt. I can choose either to play or not. I usually choose to play—even if it's a lousy hand. I keep thinking about poker. It's like poker in many ways, but it is also dissimilar. First of all, this is hardly a game. I am not hiding anything. There is some risk involved. The stakes are always high, but I would not gamble with my life, that's for sure. I might bet on the person taking care of me to do the right thing; however, this is usually an informed thought. In this respect, I have been very lucky, because there is much evidence that shows the contrary with other people.

The connotations associated with the terms "caregiver" and "assistant" are loaded for me. I wish I could be more light-hearted about this, but I can't. I have decided to call my caregivers "attendants." This term feels appropriate for me at this point.

Chapter 11

Wind Me Up and Let Me Go

THE WORLD IS ROUND AND THE PLACE WHICH MAY SEEM LIKE
THE END MAY ALSO BE THE BEGINNING.
—Ivy Baker Priest

WE MUST BE WILLING TO GET RID OF THE LIFE WE'VE PLANNED,
SO AS TO
HAVE THE LIFE THAT IS AWAITING US... THE OLD SKIN HAS TO BE
SHED BEFORE THE NEW ONE IS TO COME.
—Joseph Campbell

WHILE AT THE rehab centre, I would go with my parents and whoever was visiting me to have iced coffee drinks next door, where a major hospital had a specialty coffee shop. I began to drink liquids during the day, even with the feeding tube in place—I love coffee. I remember Joy visiting with me there the most.

There was a coffee shop in the original hospital and I remember I could not wait for the day I could have a coffee. If I had to identify a major craving, that would be it—coffee. We take the little things for granted, right?

My mom came into the hospital and rehab centre early every morning to brush my teeth, clear out my throat and rinse my mouth using a suction apparatus. This was pretty intuitive on my mom's part. As a result of breathing through my mouth, a lot of gunk collected in my throat. Lovely, eh? Doug mentioned that many people get sick while in a coma because of lack of oral hygiene. He is studying (again) to be a speech pathologist and is knowledgeable in this area. I never became ill, got an infection or pneumonia, which is common with people in comas. Remarkably, my mother's dentist in Montreal even sent her dental supplies. He actually cried when he heard I came out of the coma, so I am told.

My parents hired a caregiver for me while I was hospitalized. Betty always says that it was destiny that we met. What a lovely woman—she always made me feel capable and that I was more able than I imagined. Betty was coolness and inspiration personified. We did everyday things together in addition to the basic elements. We went shopping for clothes, saw movies and shared our favourite television show plots. Betty would help me bathe, do aesthetics and attend important appointments with me. She tells me that she initially performed Reiki[19] on me when I was in the coma and gave me energy. I believe all that is positive. Lots of people prayed for me. Some I knew; some I didn't know at all. Some were in prayer groups; others were individual. Some people lit candles; some added my name to lists of people to be healed. For instance, my mom's friend Raemali still puts my name on a prayer list that circles the globe. This is fabulous to me. I believed then, as I do now, that prayer is all good energy—whatever the denomination.

Betty says she prayed around my bed with my family. In

---

19 See <http://www.reiki.org/FAQ/WhatIsReiki.html>

my opinion, I think it is great to focus energy in a group toward a person. I was the focus for a group doing physiotherapy on me two years later. Material objects actually fell down. To me, this was an awesome sign. I made it significant, whether it was or not. I feel, especially in this case, that interpretation creates meaning. What the meaning is depends on the individual creating it. I believe that even raw data is interpretive. I mean, people look at it and decide what it means, n'est-ce pas?

For example, everyone considered Pluto a planet. Now it no longer is. Meaning and interpretation change over time. It is not that the data necessarily changes; the context does. Context can be a person or an event. Some thing or some one differs, and it affects the so-called facts. In many ways, the "facts" or data are irrelevant. I think that is why our view of history alters. It is not that certain events did not take place on certain dates; it is more about how we view these events. Our perspective can alter.

After being released from rehab, I finally got the feeding tube taken out (which did not hurt a bit). Removing the tube went against the wishes of the rehabilitation clinic staff—they feared, in addition to other things that I might aspirate while eating and drinking. I insisted, and had to sign a paper relieving them of any responsibility. I never did aspirate.

I then stayed with my parents in a Toronto hotel for three months. What a difference from the hospital and rehab centre. It was like getting out of jail, I am sure. There was a freedom to it. I was in the hospital and rehab centre for eleven months. In the hotel, I had my own room, and although I required an attendant in the mornings and evenings, there was a liberatory quality to it. We saw some wonderful plays and ate dinners in the hotel and in the vicinity. As we were very close to Toronto's Harbourfront, we went there often. It was touristy, but, as it was on the water, relaxing. I also had the opportunity to visit with my friends. Before I left, I hosted a tea party at the hotel and invited many of them. It was a send-off and a reunion at once.

My friend Mark came to see me quite a bit in the hotel as well as at the hospital. I really looked forward to his visits. Besides always having something great to say, he has tremendous energy and he is far from hard to look at. To me, he is stunning in a Brad Pitt kind of way. He is also very intelligent. Sexy and smart—what a combination! The twinkle in his eye is priceless and his smile is incredibly warming. I remember him saying that when I could not speak, he was worried that the conversations were too one-sided. Even so, it does not follow that I did not enjoy them. His mere presence was wonderful. Everything else was a bonus—like us being able to converse together. I truly always enjoyed his company.

I moved from Ontario to Quebec, from Toronto to Montreal, where my parents live, on October 12, 2004. Betty, my caregiver, came all the way from Toronto to be with me and stayed with me until June 2006. I gave up my funky apartment and my precious cat Leiloo. Come to think of it, on August 5, 2003, I just walked out of my apartment and into the hospital. I never saw my apartment or my cat Leiloo again. In a big sense, I left my life behind. I live with my parents and a caregiver for the time being. I need constant care for now. I miss living on my own. I did for more than twenty years.

One of my physiotherapists, Daniel M., asked me if I took a medical transport from Toronto to Montreal. Nope, we went in my dad's car. With assistance to sit in the front seat, I can sit there for a long trip. In the summer of 2006, I went by car for an awesome vacation, to the Shaw Festival in Niagara-on-the-Lake in Ontario (where I saw two great plays). We then drove to Ontario wine country (where I bought great wine). We ended up at Niagara Falls, which was awesome (I loved it—I got carded at an establishment there, which meant the authorities thought I was under the legal age limit to do whatever). We did the entire trip by car. It was more than fine and very comfortable. The vacation was terrific and the entire car experience felt very standard. It did from the beginning of the trip. Now, I still need help to get in, but I move more freely.

When I arrived in Montreal, I entered the Institut de Réadaptation de Montréal. For speech, we worked on articulation and other exercises; for occupational therapy, there were transfers and cognitive exercises; and for physiotherapy, there was strength training, balance work, standing, etc. I have to say learning to eat on my own in the lunchroom was the most significant for me. Up until that time, I was used to being fed by others. Betty would accompany me, as I was an outpatient, and she would encourage me to eat on my own. This, in retrospect, was major for me.

I still have physiotherapy at home every day during the week with Franc, the team leader, Daniel M. and Hélène. Franc (Francisco) runs and owns L'Équipe de Réadaptation à

Domicile (ERD). We have exercises for my fingers and arms (Proprioceptive Neuromuscular Facilitation). We do swimming pool work and, occasionally, we do Osteopathy and Myofascial work. Franc says that I am still waking up from my coma.

In many ways, I think he is right. I mean, I remember my first dream in June 2006. *It was about Madonna and I was attending her concert.* I adore Madonna. To me, her celebrity status is unique. In reality, she was giving a concert in Montreal at the time. I was invited to attend by Daniel P., but because my seat was in an unfriendly wheelchair zone, I regretfully had to decline. I did see her once with my friend Larissa, and Madonna answered on-air a question of mine that I sent via email to a music station. What a thrill that was. I asked her what kind of advice she would give to her daughter. I had her response on my answering machine for the longest time. A friend who I had not spoken to in a while caught the show, called me long-distance and wondered if it was me Madonna was responding to. One of my physiotherapists had a dream that *I met Madonna.* I would love that dream to come true.

I now carry on conversations while I do other things. I used to have to articulate every step along the way or at least think very hard about it. My mother and Franc also said I was becoming more self-aware. Even though I was able to beat people at board games and do crossword puzzles, this area of my brain seemed to take its time. Franc said my brain was busy taking care of higher functions. I guess it was problematic to multi-task. I imagine Franc was talking about stuff like breathing. Things that are still difficult for me include chewing, swallowing and talking at mealtime. I find I have to be very careful so I do not choke. Lately, I find I am using what I learn in physiotherapy and applying it to mealtime. I am obviously making new connections because none of this was intentional. I have been told to control my legs when I do certain exercises. Now when I put down a cup or a plate, I am quite gentle. I think of that exercise and apply it in a different way to a different situation. In the pool, I let the water touch my lips before holding my breath under water. Now I do the same for food, that is, I let the food touch my lips in the same way, whereas before I would use my tongue or just open my mouth. All my movements are finer now, where they used to be gross. I really notice a difference in that way.

I was discussing the topic of self-awareness the other day and, for me, self-awareness has little to do with consciousness or intelligence. There are still parts of my body I will not look at, not because I cannot but maybe I find it too distressing and distasteful. My mother thinks I should look at these parts if only to create new brain patterns with which to connect to these parts. I am conflicted by this because someone I trust has told me not to look in a mirror if it is too shocking to me. I do look in the mirror during physio, for example, when we are working on my face or eye, but what I see is constantly surprising to me. I am surrounded by photos of what I used to look like and I have all my memories of the same, so it is hard to tell if I am limiting myself because of these or what? In any case, I avoid the mirror in daily life.

Like I often say, everything I do is rehabilitation, from

smiling at my nephew (which activates my left cheek) to getting out of bed in the morning (I focus on my balance and legs). Everything I actively do seems to have an effect on my body.

My parents' friends Allan and Arlene, whom I have known for most of my life, keep sending me gifts that include the motto "Never stop moving." I heard that Arlene takes dance classes in New York City with a well-known instructor named Luigi, who, after a serious accident, was apparently told by doctors he would never walk again. Not only does he walk, but he dances. Liza Minnelli recovered from her illness with his assistance. She sent me a very lovely "get well soon" message through Allan and Arlene, who know her well. I realize it has been years since I walked, but if they could do it, so can I.

You know, it might take time before I walk again—c'est la vie. It is odd: Sometimes I feel like I am supposed to walk straight away and at other times, I feel like no one believes I will ever walk again. It is weird, but I know I will walk, although it might not be as fast as some would like. If I paid attention to the supposed "people in the know," I would not be here today, period. I figure if I could beat those odds, I can certainly walk.

Daniel M., one of my physiotherapists, does stretching (range of motion), balance and strength training with me. We do sitting balance where I try to touch his outstretched hands, standing balance in which I try to achieve symmetry, mat work (called a functional sequence) and we practice walking together, sometimes with a cane and sometimes without one. He also introduced me to a very funny French show on television that I really like and find hysterical.

Hélène works on the left side of my face—including attempting to pucker my lips and raise my left eyebrow. Hélène also facilitates my breathing and gives me massages for circulation and relaxation. We play new-age music on a CD player. My favourites are forest and water sounds accompanied by piano. Blissful.

Tamara is my independent speech pathologist—I find her incredibly supportive of me and extremely positive. In addition to articulation and soft palette exercises, we practice pitch control and talking on the telephone. She asks me conversational questions on the phone as practice for the real thing. I even pretend to order food from takeout menus that she brings in for me. The fact that I am a vegetarian makes this exercise so humorous. I do try to find food that is applicable. All my therapists are extremely talented, special, nice and funny—I laugh a lot with all of them.

Speaking of laughing or crying, I find my emotions are hard to hide these days. I am easily provoked now. I cry much quicker than I used to. Even if I do not want to, I cannot control it. Franc says this is a common after-effect that applies to several of his clients. I think I always laughed a lot, and this is hardly offensive (which is debatable, because laughter can be very cruel, too), but sometimes crying seems inappropriate. I certainly cannot stop once I start. In 2005, I laughed very loud because I could not control volume. Some neighbours nearby who could hear me actually called to complain. Of course, I just thought they were being petty, but I did feel bad for my parents, who were very understanding. I really could not believe that laughter was such an annoyance to people.

Crying really feels immature to me. I know that over time, from babyhood to adulthood, we learn to negotiate emotional responses. I hope it comes back. If not, it may take much more time to relearn. I know some people might think "Just let it be," but that is harder than it seems. I do believe that crying is very healthy, but it is not always called for. I think all I want to be able to do is regulate. I want to have a choice in the matter.

My mother says my therapists are like coaches, a description I really like. I imagine that athletes who apparently know what they are doing still have coaches. This has broadened my perspective on their role with me. Now it is not only about rehabilitation, I try to focus on the new skills they bring to my life. I am always astonished by their levels of expertise. I feel incredibly fortunate to have them in my life.

At first, I thought rehab was about relearning, which I find very tedious. My mind knows this stuff; my body just will not do what I tell it. Is this relearning? I know that practicing and repetition works for me. For instance, my signature has really improved over time. I try to work at it every day. It certainly is not that I do not know what to write or how. It is just the action that gets weird. My mom says it is like a skater learning to do the triple lutz or a swimmer learning to do a complicated dive. They have to practice. My dad made the analogy of a piano player who has a piano but does not know the piece to be played. The piano will not play by itself. But my "instrument" is broken. So even if I learn the piece, something will be off. I really feel that another analogy made by my mom is quite appropriate for me. She mentioned that a baby who is born with eyes but is kept in a dark room will not see.

If I am using new brain connections to do certain things that I already know how to do, then it is relearning, which is so important, obviously. I need to teach these pathways to take over from the old ones. It is all a concept and a half to me.

I had foot surgery—to help me walk again—in June 2005. The doctor had to do a tendon transfer and an Achilles tendon lengthening. During the coma, my left foot went into a funny position with my toes pointed down. Called "dropped foot," it needed to be corrected. (Like I said, there are tons of surgical procedures now.) I tried to fix it in physiotherapy and with braces, but nothing worked. It still does not feel like the right foot, but it sure looks good. In addition to trying to negotiate the mixed-up signals to my brain with respect to balance and coordination, I have to negotiate this foot. It feels like it is turning, and there is some numbness on the bottom. Right now, a foot brace has been created for me that I wear all of the time. This brace prevents my foot from pointing down and also makes daily activity more comfortable. I look forward to the day when I can wear regular shoes again. For now, one shoe has to be bigger than the other.

I really think I became much more aware mentally because of the pain that followed my foot surgery. I am definitely not advocating pain as therapy. For instance while I was in a coma, I was poked and prodded in an attempt to get a reaction out of me. Pain, for me, is determined by circumstance and time.

Morphine did not work very well after the foot surgery. As my mother says, "Imagine if you hadn't even had that!" Betty stayed with me all night and held my hand. I surrounded myself in white healing light. I believe that really worked. I had very little swelling and my scars are pretty minimal.

I used to think about getting a tattoo—an Aztec sun—right where the incision for the Achilles tendon lengthening is. I never got the tattoo. The only thing holding me back is the knowledge that they do not bury people with tattoos in Jewish cemeteries, and I had decided a while ago that that is where I want to be buried.

In another dream, *a friend was burying me in a Jewish cemetery. She was looking for an appropriate headstone and a Jewish newspaper to put in a notice.*

I do not, and did not, consider this dream a nightmare or morbid at all. I know many people are scared of death. As you know, I am not.

Chapter 12

Before

EDUCATION IS AN ADMIRABLE THING, BUT IT IS WELL TO
REMEMBER FROM TIME TO TIME THAT NOTHING THAT IS WORTH
KNOWING CAN BE TAUGHT.
—Oscar Wilde

TO LIVE IS SO STARTLING IT LEAVES LITTLE TIME FOR ANYTHING
ELSE.
—Emily Dickinson

EVEN THOUGH MY views on the body are unique and although I am relatively unscathed by my current physical status, there is a "before" and "after" quality to the life I am leading. Before, I could walk, I could talk and sound like people expected, I could write by hand, reading was much easier, I could drive, and I could dance, swim and sing. It is not like you forget those things. I may have adapted well to my situation, but I do have my memories. I suppose if I were born this way, then I would have no comparison. But I do. I am not making a judgment; I am stating what was for me.

Many people say I have already lived a lot in this lifetime. I am sure that is part of the reason I am relatively unconflicted now. I lived in Paris, France and went to the Sorbonne for an independent course on French culture after getting my B.A.

in English at McGill University in Montreal. When I was in Paris, I would cut class to see exhibits of photographs. I even bought books that had these images. At the time, I was really into graffiti, so most of my photos are about these. To me, they were urban works of art. I was able to find a lot near subway stops. The artists were anonymous, so I could reflect on the work without the distraction of personality. I am still glad I did not take any pictures of tourist spots or familiar destinations, like the Eiffel Tower. What I did shoot reminds me of who I was at the time. As usual, it was far from conventional. These pictures are of "my" Paris.

I took a large-format printing class with my favourite photographer, Edward Burtynsky, about a year before I went into the hospital. His work not only speaks to me, but sends shivers through me. I remember I couldn't afford to buy his prints, so I would frame gallery invitations with his work on them. I had a newspaper print of his work on a bulletin board for the longest time. My current bedroom view is of huge, old grain silos; beyond that is downtown Montreal and beyond that, a mountain. What an awesome comment on how we transform our landscape. To many people, the silos are an "eyesore" blocking their view. To me, they are a beautiful obstruction. I could look at them all day. They are the view. I took a picture of the view from the same bedroom "before" and would look at it every day. It stayed on my desk in Toronto. Like Edward Burtynsky says, this is a manufactured landscape.

I am drawn to images that warp or distort reality. I always loved "experimental" films. I once took a class "illegally" just to see the out-of-the-ordinary films—I was not graded on it, but I probably learned the most I ever did. Maya Deren's 1943 film *Meshes of the Afternoon* still haunts me. The unusual is spectacular to me. I know this fascination seeps into other areas of my life. I am certain that is why I wrote my doctoral dissertation on drag. Taking the ordinary and making it extraordinary is not only a challenge, but it is wondrous. Difference is essential to breaking down convention and it is unique. It is something to be valued, not avoided. Most everyone wants to fit in. I say stand out. You might face huge amounts of opposition. So it takes courage to be different. Be brave.

I guess "living a lot" included living all over the place. I lived in two different places in Canada—Montreal, Quebec and Toronto, Ontario. I sang on tape, CD, video and live. I acted in plays (a play was written for me), television (I was in a series where I had the opportunity to play a young mother—the director said my "daughter" and I could be sisters, but I still got the part) and film (the auditions were the best part). I met some amazing directors, like Robert Altman. I worked at various jobs: teaching, public relations, film business and coverage—I would review new scripts for a producer. The job I had before my brain surgery was great; unfortunately, I was constantly tired. I was the Communications Director for an animation school. In addition to being mega-organized, I realized I was technology-abled. I remember I had to set up some new cellphones. I just read the manual and ta-da. The heads were in the process of making an animation film, so I worked on that, too. Right before the brain surgery, I took an animation voice-over class that I absolutely adored. I also studied French, wrote articles and was a voice in an animation film. Sure, you're thinking, I should have been tired even without the brain thing. I found all this work invigorating and stimulating.

After a really bad breakup (are there any good kinds?), I remember that I took a road trip by myself from Los Angeles to San Francisco. This may sound pompous, but I thought to myself on my hotel bed, I could go for an Oscar or Ph.D. My conclusion was that it would be much less subjective to get the degree. I have a Ph.D.—I am an expert on gender, drama and film. This degree came after my Masters in drama at the University of Toronto (Graduate Centre for the Study of Drama). Time passes anyhow, I thought I might as well get some degrees.

I attended conferences everywhere, but I have to say I loved New York City the most. I gave a paper at a cinema studies conference and did tons of sightseeing as well. I went to New York City with my friend Shelley. She is now a university professor; she's Buddhist, has bright red hair and is very talented. We did things like go to Tiffany's. For me, it was visiting the place they filmed *Breakfast at Tiffany's* (Blake Edwards, 1961). It was all so wonderful to me. I bought Tiffany's stationery with the monogram R that I still have. It is an amazing souvenir, which I wanted to save, and it was hard to use for that reason. We did many things, most of which required money. We ate cheesecake at Saks and dined at the Chandelier Room at the Tavern on the Green. I bought a large stuffed teddy bear for myself at FAO Schwartz, which I remember schlepping back on the plane, and we went to the Russian Tearoom, where, in a very glam way, I drank champagne. We danced at an "alternative" nightclub I wanted to check out and we listened to a big band in very small quarters. Shelley and I saw *Damn Yankees* on Broadway, attended a taping of *Late Night with Conan O'Brian* and rode the subway. We stayed with an old school friend who brought us fresh bagels in the morning and showed us around.

I flew to Las Vegas for a popular culture conference and, like I tell my friend Mark, it was so "meta." It was a microcosm of culture to me. It made perfect sense that a popular culture conference was held there. I remember they were just building the Paris Las Vegas resort at the time. My brother Warren helped me with the video portion of my presentation. It was received very well and was fun to do. My presentation was on k.d. lang, who was named Miss Chatelaine, and I showed Lawrence Welk videos—bubbles and all. I once saw k.d. lang give a brilliant concert in Quebec City on my way to Prince Edward Island. At a special book sale in Las Vegas, I bought a book on the science of *Star Trek*. Oh. My. God.

I used to go camping as much as I could. I remember that the sunlight in Prince Edward Island seemed really special to me. I thought if God made a heaven, this light would be used. Needless to say, this is one of my favourite spots on Earth, and I have done a lot of travelling. To me, Prince Edward Island is completely magical. So it makes perfect sense to me that most of my dreams are set in nature.

I had lovers and long-term relationships. I even had a great love—something many people do not have in their life. I miss kissing a lot. I have trouble puckering and blending my lips now. Chemistry with a person is the most important thing.

I definitely have issues about getting into a relationship presently. These include, but go way beyond, the physical aspect—although that is certainly a part of it. Image for me is problematic. Funny, I really do not care about it in other people, but for me it is important. I do believe in physical attraction, but that is different from physical attractiveness. I probably had to deal with my perspective before, but now it is really highlighted. Self-reflection can be quite revealing. I do crave to be with someone I care about; I just hope I let myself.

It is emotionally very difficult to think you are going to be with somebody and then that does not come to fruition. The hope of "forever" makes it worse. Even though I try to get away from "expectation," I realize I am full of expectation. Expectation is like a fairy tale. It is seldom based in reality and is more akin to wish fulfillment. We talk of fairy-tale marriages, for instance. Is "hope" grounded in "the real"? Does that even matter? Maybe "hope" is closer to faith: a belief in the intangible. I enjoy the idea of "hope" being ephemeral.

I made a decision "just to be." "Authenticity" was a dirty word when I was studying it. Maybe I am thinking of "essentialism." Despite the ramifications, I will try to be as true to who I think I am as possible. You know, it is so hard, and I wish I could just let go, but I have to be "strong." Strength requires energy. So "just being" means holding that up as well. To me, these qualities are not opposites. There is an integration that is not dichotomous. This weaving of identity is a huge challenge for most. To me, it is about "blending."

Something is happening. I am letting go of that which does not work for me. I know I have changed; I guess I am accommodating that change. It is less of an intolerance and more of a shift. It could be my neurology or simply aging. I think I have more self-respect. I just do not resonate as I used to with some familiar people and events. It is like a metamorphoses of "self."

These days I am focusing mostly on my rehab, but I do go out to see films, plays, concerts, operas and museums. Pretty fabulous, eh? I feel very fortunate to do this.

You know, I do not have any regrets at present about what I chose to do, pretty much because I did what I set out to do. Not that I will not do other things now, but what if I had never sang? What if I had never swam? I have had those experiences in my life; no one can take that away from me. It might seem weird, but these aspects being severely diminished do not make me long for or miss them.

In this dream, *I was an Inuit doctor on a plane heading for Toronto. It was so colourful, vivid and real. I was a doctor trying to save a young boy on the plane. My mother was there. We were all heading for Toronto because we felt that there would be better medical facilities there for the boy. Through the windows, there was a gorgeous sunset of many hues on snow-capped mountain peaks. When we were in Toronto, we flew very low over Bloor Street.* I remember that I was female and had long straight black hair. I have curly hair.

Interestingly, Franc brought this to my attention: In all of my dreams, I was always female. I was "me" but often different nationalities. Hmmm.

Chapter 13

C'est la Vie

AFTER I MOVED to Montreal, I became an aunt for the first time. Yipee! My brother Doug is the father, and Sonya is the mother. Eli Keese Shiller was born on July 20, 2005. I feel so honoured just to be around. Having a child or children is an awesome thing. It is a major experience I have not had. Many people say that having kids is overrated. I could not disagree more. I truly believe children are special beings; most of them just need an opportunity to express themselves. I am looking forward to the day I can ask Eli stuff and he can respond. I am sure my experience in the hospital will be relatable. At the same time, he might not remember what he went through. I did not speak or walk, I wore diapers and food was an issue. Communicating need was awkward and often unsuccessful.

The thing is, even though I was brought back to an infantile state, I was an adult. Especially now, I am able to reflect upon the entire experience with an adult mind. How many of us get the chance to do that? It might have been very bizarre and uncomfortable, but there is an opportunity here for serious consideration. For me, now, this can add to my empathy and influence how I think. At the time, I was in the moment with all these experiences. But now, as memories, they enable a different process. I guess it's about how you look at it.

Sonya had her baby shower in May 2005, and I really thought I could handle the whole experience. Emotionally, though, I could not. Most of the people there had not seen me since Doug and Sonya's wedding in 2002. Many had preconceptions about my present state, so it seemed. Some did not even say "Hi" to me. Some of those who did were extremely condescending. Fortunately, I had invited a couple of friends, Joy and Sylvie, who were very supportive of me.

I could not help but feel guilty for living. Sonya and her brother and sister lost their mother to a brain tumour. I could not stop thinking about that. Their profound loss, so close to my situation, really impacted my entire experience. It was difficult to feel joyful with the thought of their grief. I thought I must be a horrific reminder of an unbearable event. To lose a mother, how absolutely horrid: so much pain and sadness. Sonya was about to become a mother herself. The mother theme was highlighted. I did not want to be responsible for negative emotions.

And then, there was Cameron, Sonya's little nephew, whom I became friends with at my brother's wedding.

Cameron thought I did not remember him. Of course, I did. This really bothered me. To be quite honest, I was very shy and extremely self-conscious in addition to having conflicting emotions. I probably did not present myself well at all. We both changed physically, but intrinsically, I believe we are the same people. He might be too young to realize this, but as I said, many adults felt uncomfortable with me. C'est la vie, I guess. I will never forget how much Cameron meant to me so quickly. I have no doubt he will grow up to be a fine person. I hope to reconnect with him at some future point. Sonya's baby shower was definitely not the place or time.

Chapter 14

Queasy

IT TAKES A LOT OF COURAGE TO RELEASE THE FAMILIAR AND
SEEMINGLY SECURE, TO EMBRACE THE NEW. BUT THERE IS NO
REAL SECURITY IN WHAT IS NO LONGER MEANINGFUL. THERE IS
MORE SECURITY IN THE ADVENTUROUS AND EXCITING, FOR IN
MOVEMENT THERE IS LIFE, AND IN CHANGE THERE IS POWER.
—Alan Cohen

RESISTANCE IS FUTILE.
—*THE BORG, FROM THE TELEVISION SERIES STAR TREK: THE NEXT
GENERATION*

I HEARD THAT Che Guevera said something about surviving
an illness being revolutionary. I really like the idea of my
recovery being like a revolution. I guess the way my mind
works is pretty revolutionary. I do not think like most people
I know, that's for sure. By many standards, I am pretty un-
conventional. My actions speak for themselves. Two things
I can think of right off the bat are that I am unmarried and
I do not have kids. Not that I do not want either, but they
obviously have not been a priority for me. I was never the
kind of girl who dreamt of her wedding day. Having a stable
partner is very nice, but I never thought I would need to get
married to have that. I remember when I was eight years

old, a little boy asked me to marry him. I got queasy. I know we were too young to get married, but I cannot shrug this feeling that I was hard-wired for resistance early on. In any case, I do believe we have our personalities from birth. We get shaped by, or react to, our experiences.

I usually don't care what others think of me. Sure, I get disappointed, but I really try not to judge anyone. I am probably much harder on myself than I am with others.

In February 2006, I saw a plastic surgeon about the left side of my face. I wanted symmetry. He basically told me nothing could be done without major surgery, which I refuse to have. They would have to remove a muscle from my inner thigh and move it to my cheek. Also, they might put something in my left eyelid to make it more symmetrical with the right eye. Yikes! What a disappointment it was for me. I know that people have facelifts and implants all of the time. Someone will just have to accept me as I am. I really cannot imagine that this surgery would improve my physicality. To me, it's all about vanity.

I also saw an audiologist who tested my hearing, which is apparently excellent. Oddly enough, when I shut my left eye, I feel like I get more information or layers of sound from waterfalls or rushing water and air conditioners. Like Hélène (one of my therapists) says, there are lots of muscles between the eye and ear. What I infer from that is that a connection of some sort is being made. The audiologist heard lots of noise in my left ear. I guess certain signals are getting crossed.

I have heard from a few people that what I say about the lack of correspondence between my mind and my body is what aged people say. That is, my mind does not correspond to my body. What an opportunity to not only empathize, but to actually experience what other people go through. The possibilities for this kind of event are really quite stunning.

It bugs me that I am perceived of as mentally challenged because of how I look or sound. If I were mentally challenged, then I imagine that would be that, but I am not. Again, we get to the idea of preconceptions. I am aware that these have been around since time immemorial, used against many groups of people. I think that because I had brain surgery, many people assume my intelligence has been affected. This is so wrong—I cannot even begin to tell you. I understand the assumption, but it is false. Also, I think that because my physicality has been affected, there is a presumption that the way I think has changed, too. My brother Warren says that people only need to talk with me a little while to know this is not true. What a bummer, though.

Stereotypes seem to be a foundation for civilization. Personally I do not think it has to be this way, but it is all many people know. The understanding of it does not diminish its impact. Unfortunate but very real for me, I feel the impact of prejudice all the time: in different forms, from people I do not know to people I love. I know people who would freak out if "prejudice" were levied against them, yet they are guilty of it themselves. I do not think it is about hypocrisy; some people are just ignorant of what they are doing. I know this has nothing to do with intelligence. Some very smart people can act in very dehumanizing ways. People who imagine they are beyond prejudice can be stunned by their own, inadvertent belief system. It can be astonishing to see how we react to certain circumstances. It is my belief that if we pay attention, we can learn something about ourselves. We might not like what we see. If so, we can change. It might be really hard to be honest with yourself. There is much value in truth. I cannot imagine doing all this in one sitting. I am pretty sure you need time to absorb, to process. It might take a lifetime.

There are obvious prejudices, for example, against skin colour, but there are subtle ones as well, involving gender and sexuality. Sometimes we see nothing at all. Usually this could include poverty or background (or sexuality, etc.). Not seeing a difference, you could make automatic assumptions—about one's actions, for example. It is very necessary to validate the invisible. Some people, like disabled persons, have been made invisible; ignored. It means so much, in this case, to be seen. Historically, some laws have been established to deal with the repercussions of being seen. In the United States of America, there was an "Ugly Law." This is how the Chicago Municipal Law read before its repeal: "No person who is diseased, maimed, mutilated or in any way deformed so as to be an unsightly or disgusting object or improper person to be allowed in or on the public ways or other public places in this city, or shall therein or thereon expose himself to public view, under a penalty of not less than one dollar nor more than fifty dollars for each offense."[20]

Obviously, not everything is prejudice. We are certainly al-

---

20 See < http://www.zmag.org/content/showarticle.
   cfm?ItemID=2583>

lowed to have opinions about things. What I am concerned with is the harmful effects of these opinions. This is not about being politically correct or contrary; it's about disrupting lives with the negative impact of these opinions. It can be, and usually is, harmful. I think the term "prejudice" itself has specific connotations associated with it. Understandably, most people would abhor (I hope) an affiliation with this term, so it could be very difficult to examine your relationship to it. I think it would take so much self-awareness and a willingness to search deep. If all this sounds tiring, I imagine we could all live an unexamined life, but I can't see the benefit in that. It takes work and it takes effort to be self-reflective. I really think it is worthwhile.

Chapter 15

Aha!

NOT TO KNOW IS BAD. NOT TO WISH TO KNOW IS WORSE.
—Proverb

YOU HAVE TO CHOOSE WHERE YOU LOOK, AND IN MAKING THAT
CHOICE YOU ELIMINATE ENTIRE WORLDS.
—Barbara Bloom

UNFORTUNATELY, IT BOTHERS me that people make false assumptions about me. But really, what can I do? I certainly cannot control what other people think. I guess I wish they were better informed. I know I was not. I took tons for granted: like communication, for example. Some people just have a harder time speaking than others do. It does not need to mean more than that. Aha! Their mind might know what they want to say; they just have a difficult time articulating ideas. Who knew?

Some people wonder if I feel blessed or cursed. I truly feel blessed. I was never the kind of person who asked "Why me?" I will not be like that now, no matter how understandable it would be. I was never one to take the easy road and I really believe that I understand the concept of "margin-

ר

alization"[21] very well. So, in some ways, this feels familiar. Would I change my physical state? You bet. But I actually have learned from this whole ordeal and I do continue to change physically. I choose to view this as a learning experience. So, this does feel like a gift to me in many ways. It may suck at times, but usually, I try to see the benefits. This does not mean I ever gave up; it is simply that I accept where I am for now. There is much I cannot stand, but there is more I can stand and that I am willing to bear.

So, I guess I see the glass as half full. I see the liquid in the glass rather than the empty part. It's called "selective perception."[22] It is inadvertently how I cope. I am not always happy, but I do manage.

You know, the "challenges" that people now complain about are those I wish I had. It is not that I do not get how difficult some things can be for some people. Everything is relative, after all—but really. So-called challenges are so different and difficult for me now: like taxes or even writing this book. I do it, but only because I set my mind to the task at hand. Believe me, it is all full of effort on my part. My typing is not great, but I try to do a bit every day. When I was in grade eight at Town of Mount Royal High School, I took a typing class with the tiny but very determined Mrs. Katz, so thankfully I know where all the letters are. I now use one very compromised finger to type this book when I used to use both hands freely to type anything. So, sure, this

---

21 See <http://en.wikipedia.org/wiki/Marginalization>
22 See <http://www.ciadvertising.org/student_account/fall_01/adv382j/howardmo/whatissp.html>

Aha!

is a challenge, but I really like it and I am more than willing to take it on. Some things, like taxes, you just have to do. It may not be fun or easy, but you do it anyway. That is the way it goes, eh? It is ironic, but even taxes feel like a luxury to me.

Another thing that bothers me is that people close to me have an opportunity to learn from my experience and yet, unfortunately, I do not see much growth. Growth can happen on a spiritual and/or physical level (in addition to others, of course). Often, both levels are intertwined. It's so odd, and this might sound harsh, but those who profess to be extremely spiritual seem to be the least. That old cliché does ring true: I guess actions do speak louder than words. Maybe others wish I were the way I was. If I do not feel sorry for myself and if I am willing to make an effort, I really do not get what the problem is. I am presently dependent on other people for some assistance. It is very difficult for me to have to deal with others' issues as well as my own. As was recently brought to my attention, I am very well adjusted, maybe more so than those around me. Understanding this does not ease my frustration. I think that I am pretty compassionate, but there are certain things I have little tolerance for.

I like to talk about things, like how I feel, for instance. I know that not everybody is like that. Some people like to sweep stuff under the rug. If people imagine they are protecting me by not bringing things up, well, it is having the opposite effect.

Epilogue, Part 1

Like Watching Grass Grow

THAT IS HAPPINESS; TO BE DISSOLVED INTO SOMETHING
COMPLETELY GREAT.
—Willa Cather

CONFIDENCE IS A PLANT OF SLOW GROWTH IN AN AGED BOSOM.
—William Pitt, Earl of Chatham

I AM CONTINUING to "heal." Like my dad says, it's "like watching grass grow." The process of physical recovery is very slow. I can stand and walk with help—usually a physiotherapist's help. I will continue to have physiotherapy every day if I need it. My goal is to walk without assistance. My problem is not strength, which I have, but balance. I do not wear a foot brace any longer; I now wear my old sneakers, which are so much lighter. The bonus is I can now wear two identical shoes. Coincidently, my mom found and ordered winter boots for me on the Internet. The model of the boot is called "Romy"—I rarely see my name on a product. Weird and wonderful! They are so cute and I cannot wait to wear them. The colours are great for me—black and pink—they are very warm and light as well. I feel I was destined to get them.

I sometimes expect to wake up in a medical institution. Like in that *Buffy* episode, I do at times think that I am in an institution somewhere and I am dreaming all of this. In *The X-Files* (which first aired September 10, 1993 and ended May 19, 2002), they say, "Dreams are answers to questions we haven't yet figured out how to ask." At times, all of this really does feel like a dream. The reality of having survived brain surgery and a lengthy coma is truly full of meaning to me. The resulting hardships seem benign in comparison. I sometimes think of what could have been if things had stayed the same as they were. I believe we tell ourselves stories: They can be the "If only I had known." Hindsight is 20/20, so who knows. I would not change a thing I had actually done—everything has made me who I am today—the good and the bad. If I could have, I think I would have had kids. But this would have been so hard on them, and much more difficult on me. I guess that was not my path. In the future, maybe I will adopt. We shall see what happens. To me, the unknown is quite exciting. I do not find it scary at all. To be quite honest, I look forward to it. Things may not be all pretty and neat, but according to me, that is all right.

I have been asked if I am Buddhist. I am not. Although my sensibilities might be aligned with a particular group, I feel no need to belong to a particular group. I was born Jewish and I intend to stay Jewish. I cannot be swayed or convinced otherwise. This might appear stubborn. I do not fit into a standard model of a Jew (if there is such a thing), but then again, I do not fit into any dominant ideas of anything. I am comfortable being an anomaly. I have been called a witch by some people. I think of *The Wizard of Oz* and my grandparents. My usual reply is that if so, "I am a good witch." I would have been burnt at the stake or in the ovens no matter what. In *Buffy*, there were a couple of witches who were magical beyond their special abilities. Even though they were fictional characters, I am more than honoured to be put in the same category as them. They certainly were not the scary representations of witches. They looked so regular. They must have changed some minds about the evil spookiness of witches.

The witch in *Buffy* who would/could not stop doing magic was treated like an addict. The storyline really blew me away. I had never seen anything like it. Everyone involved must have been so brave. To me, this was innovation and subversion in a popular format. What a concept!

Oddness does not bother me like it bothers some people. The so-called strange is simply not strange to me. It is not that I think other people are wrong; I just listen to my own sensibility. I trust it.

My legacy is resistance; everything I do and think reflects that. I know that people have a hard time figuring me out. Maybe I am just used to it, but I expect it. I do not ever feel like the onus is on me to make myself more understood. I usually feel like I am clear enough.

My physicality is so different now. I imagine if things had stayed the same, there would have been more of the same. I am all for change. My experience now is distinct from before. I look at leggy women trying to pick up guys in a bar, and I know that this act is not for me. It can be fun, I am sure, but was it ever for me? What would I do with the option? My new physicality forces me to look beyond the box, beyond the obvious. It is very hard now, but it is an amazing lesson. To be honest, while I am certain some are very smart and nice, I would rather be me with my limited abilities than those leggy women in the bar.

I am pretty much an open book. People can ask me anything and I will answer them. I have nothing to hide. There is so much freedom in this. My answers might make some uncomfortable, but, hey, c'est la vie! And I do believe in privacy; it is just that most subjects are not taboo or off limits to me.

Epilogue, Part 2

Que Sera Sera

History has demonstrated that the most notable winners usually encountered heartbreaking obstacles before they triumphed. They won because they refused to become discouraged by their defeats.
—B.C. Forbes

My will shall shape the future. Whether I fail or succeed shall be no man's doing but my own. I am the force; I can clear any obstacle before me or I can be lost in the maze. My choice; my responsibility; win or lose, only I hold the key to my destiny.
—Elaine Maxwell

I CONTINUE TO change, which is awesome to me and very exciting. Not everybody recognizes this change: It's up to me to mention it. Although this can be quite tiring for me, the alternative is to be treated as I was. The only one who can truly suffer here is me. Conversely, some people think I am "better" than I actually am, so it is a bit of a balancing act. I do have to be incredibly aware of others' expectations of me. For instance, I was served dessert in a smaller bowl than I usually use. My mother immediately suggested we use a bigger one. I let it be known I wanted to try the smaller one. It worked out very well, and I would not have known if

I had not tried. So much for expectations: It was a pleasant surprise for her and me.

I met Bonnie Sherr Klein at the Festival des Films du Monde in Montreal in 2006 (the 30th Montreal World Film Festival). I used to go to the Toronto International Film Festival quite a bit. It was pricey for me, but I love films. It was worth every penny. I remember going early in the morning. I would have a coffee while I watched films—coffee and films, my favourite things. What a delightful treat for me! There were so many stars, directors, producers, etc. who attended this festival that I felt glamorous just being there. I went to opening and closing parties, and premieres. I remember Colin Farrell smoking outside a screening before he was well-known; I sat behind the Weinsteins at a Kevin Smith (he was there, too) film; I attended a screening with Kim Basinger and Kevin Spacey; I saw a rough cut of Eminem's film before it was finished. In the lineups before each film, I had great conversations and made new friends. There was always an excitement, spin and buzz in the air. I may sound like an entertainment show or someone doing public relations for the festival, but it was glitzy and glossy, unreal and an event. It was bigger than life and otherworldly. Even though the tickets were purchased, there was a feeling of privilege simply to be an attendee.

Bonnie Sherr Klein made a film on disabled people called *SHAMELESS: The ART of Disability* (2006), which I saw in Montreal. I remember studying her and her film, *Not a Love Story: A Film About Pornography* (1981), at McGill, "a long time ago in a galaxy far, far away" (*Star Wars*, 1977). She had a stroke several years ago, had brain surgery and still managed to make this film. She is a definite new inspiration for me. It must be difficult to make a film generally, but when you are disabled you have to wrestle with external and internal demons. Being suddenly disabled is traumatic on so many levels.

David, one of the disabled people she profiles in the film, says that a disabled person could take a dump and that would be considered "inspirational." To me, at any rate, this film is quite an accomplishment. I believe that the film is niche-oriented in that it speaks to a certain kind of disabled person, but it did speak to me in many ways. For one, Klein had a hard time looking in the mirror, like me. After seeing David's face in the film, I realized mine is not so complex. I might be used to looking a certain way, but that is all it is: convention and habit. It is still very difficult, but it's so good to know I am not alone in this feeling and action. Even though most of my current disabilities were not reflected in the film, I still felt included. There were certain commonalities: a wheelchair, for example. One of the women profiled used a computer to write, but she had a program that enabled her to talk to it. What I learned from this was that truly if you have the will, you will find a way. The film made me imagine that I was much more capable than I realized. In a sense, it opened more doors for me. That in itself is pretty amazing.

I am more than glad to be a comfort to people—if they let me. I am not a doormat; I certainly do not wish to be used. I am no martyr. What I think I have is insight, which I am more than happy to share. I do not want anyone to feel sorry for me now. I do not want pity. I do want respect, compassion, empathy.

Time is an interesting notion. In 2003 I was diagnosed with a child's brain tumour—I am too old for this diagnoses. In 2007 I was diagnosed with cataracts in my eyes—I am too young for this diagnoses. I have been told by casting-directors and directors that I look younger than appropriate age roles. I was carded by Security in Niagara Falls for appearing under-age. In many ways my body does not obey the laws of time, of age.

I guess time will tell what happens to me. As it ought to be, many people have moved on with their lives. Certain friendships have changed. This is usual; it is expected. While I have adapted to my present situation, and although my new focus is on physiotherapy, I am stuck somewhat in the past. My memories mean the world to me. In many ways, the people that I knew and the events that I participated in are still a big part of my life. In this respect, I am still in "suspended animation." "Time" is so unhinged in my philosophy that I guess this could be expected. We are governed by physical laws, but I do believe we are somewhat free to think what we like.

Our minds are constrained by things like ideology and societal pressure, which is why I think resistance is so necessary. Even my "disabilities" can resist expectation. No one said any of this would be easy; it definitely takes at the minimum an awareness, a consciousness. Some people resist expectation unintentionally, so it would be up to the witness to attach meaning. I am not radical; it's just that what I think seems not to be the standard.

Some people really want to fit in. I understand this desire, but I have never felt that way. I really don't mind being an outcast or being on the fringe. In fact, I find it preferable. I like being on the edge, at a new frontier. I want to "boldly go where no one has gone before" (*Star Trek: The Next Generation*). My earliest memories are of television re-runs of *Star Trek* (the series) and the film *Planet of the Apes* (1968, Franklin J. Schaffner). The first person I was compared to was "Mona Lisa." These influences are part of what shaped me and still maintain a part of my life.

I do not take much for granted anymore and although I do not feel an urgency about things, I will articulate more of how I feel, more than I used to. Again, this might make people uncomfortable, but it takes way too much energy to hold back.

I saw Cameron, Sonya's nephew, about a year after the baby shower. Aside from the fact that it was great to see him, I was thrilled to observe that we still have a connection. I was tentative and self-conscious at first, but that dissolved away quickly. All I thought about was my love for him and that it really would not matter if he felt the opposite for me.

I really don't know what the future holds for me. Who does? Que sera sera, right? In all cases, I do know that I can count on myself and that that in itself is something. Psychic or not, trust in yourself is formidable. I trust my intuition and gut; none of this is magic. Maybe it is more feeling than anything else.

I am moving into my own place now, near the Atwater Market and the Lachine Canal. I am still with an attendant, but it's a major step. I plan to get a cat as well as an aquarium.

Even though where I am living is more than fine, I am looking forward to my own space. I am thinking this really is a launching pad (no pun intended). My hope is that I will continue to change, learn and grow.

LIST OF WORKS CITED
FILMS AND TELEVISION

SOURCES: IMDB HTTP://WWW.IMDB.COM and the NFB Collection http://www.nfb.ca

- *Breakfast at Tiffany's.* Dir. Blake Edwards. Perfs. Audrey Hepburn, George Peppard, Patricia Neal, Buddy Epson, Jurow-Shepherd. 5 October 1961 (USA).
- *Buffy the Vampire Slayer,* the television series. Creator: Joss Whedon. Perfs. Sarah Michelle Gellar, Nicholas Brendon, Alyson Hannigan, Anthony Head. 20th Century Fox Television.1997-2003.

- *Dark City.* Dir. Alex Proyas. Perfs. Rufus Sewell, William Hurt, Kiefer Sutherland, Jennifer Connelly. Mystery Clock Cinema. 27 February 1998 (USA).

- *Groundhog Day.* Dir. Harold Ramis. *Perfs,* Bill Murray, Andie MacDowell, Chris Elliott, Stephen Tobolowsky. Columbia Pictures Corporation. 12 February 1993 (USA).

- *Lost,* the television series. Creators: J.J. Abrams, Jeffrey Lieber, Damon Lindelof. Perfs. Naveen Andrews, Josh Holloway, Daniel Dae Kim, Yunjin Kim. ABC Studios. 2 October 2004 (Canada).

- *M*A*S*H,* the television series. *Dirs.* HY AVERBACK, JACKIE COOPER etc. Perfs. ALAN ALDA, LORETTA SWIT, JAMIE FARR, WILLIAM CHRISTOPHER. 20TH CENTURY FOX TELEVISION . 1972-1983.

- *Meshes of the Afternoon.* Dirs. MAYA DEREN, ALEXANDER HAMMID. Perfs. MAYA DEREN, ALEXANDER HAMMID. 1943.

- *Not a Love Story: A Film About Pornography* . Dir. Bonnie Sherr Klein. Perfs. Linda Lee Tracey, Bonnie Klein, Suze Randall, Kate Millett. National Film Board of Canada (NFB). 1981.

- *Planet of the Apes.* Dir. Franklin J. Schaffner. Perfs. Charlton Heston, Roddy McDowall, Kim Hunter, Maurice Evans. APJAC Productions. April 1968 (USA).

- *SHAMELESS: The ART of Disability.* Dir. Bonnie Sherr Klein. Perfs. Persimmon Blackbridge, Catherine Frazee, Geoff McMurchy, David Roche. National Film Board of Canada Production. 2006.

- *Sliding Doors.* Dir. Peter Howitt. Perfs. Gwyneth Paltrow, John Hannah, John Lynch, Jeanne Tripplehorn. Intermedia Films. 24 April 1998 (USA).

- *Star Trek,* the television series. Creator: Gene Roddenberry. Perfs. Leonard Nimoy, William Shatner, DeForest Kelley,

Nichelle Nichols. Desilu Productions. 1966 -1969.

- *Star Trek: The Next Generation,* the television series. Creator: Gene Roddenberry. Perfs. Patrick Stewart, Jonathan Frakes, LeVar Burton, Marina Sirtis. Paramount Television. 1987—1994.

- *Star Wars.* Dir. George Lucas. Mark Hamill, Harrison Ford, Carrie Fisher, Peter Cushing. Lucasfilm. 1977.

- *The Matrix.* Dirs. Andy Wachowski, Larry Wachowski. Perfs. Keanu Reeves, Laurence Fishburne, Carrie-Anne Moss, Hugo Weaving. Groucho II Film Partnership.1999.

- *"The Twilight Zone, the television series. Creator: Rod Serling.*
  Perfs: Rod Serling, et al.Cayuga Productions. 1959-1964. "

- *The X-Files,* the television series. Creator: Chris Carter. Perfs. Gillian Anderson, David Duchovny, Mitch Pileggi, Robert Patrick. 20th Century Fox Television. September 10, 1993 - May 19, 2002.

MAGAZINES

- Shiller, Romy. *Fab Magazine,* No. 195, August 1-14, 2002, pp. 118-120.

WEBSITES

- http://en.thinkexist.com
- http://en.wikipedia.org/wiki/Lucien_Bouchard
- http://en.wikipedia.org/wiki/Jean_Chr%C3%A9tien
- http://en.wikipedia.org/wiki/Che_Guevara
- http://en.wikipedia.org/wiki/Locked-In_syndrome
- http://en.wikipedia.org/wiki/Marginalization
- http://en.wikipedia.org/wiki/Myofascial_Releasehttp://en.thinkexist.com
- http://simple.wikipedia.org/wiki/Pierre_Trudeau
- http://en.wikipedia.org/wiki/Terri_Schiavo
- http://en.wikipedia.org/wiki/The_Holocaust
- http://thinkexist.com/quotes/sent-by/tequisia69
- http://www.brainyquote.com
- http://www.cdc.gov/NCIDOD/SARS
- http://www.ciadvertising.org/student_account/fall_01/adv382j/howardmo/whatissp.html
- http://www.cindyjackson.com
- http://www.creativegrowth.com/johnbio.htm
- http://www.quotedb.com/quotes/668
- http://www.reiki.org/FAQ/WhatIsReiki.html
- http://www.rxlist.com/cgi/generic/heparin.htm
- http://www.startrek.com/startrek/view/index.htm
- http://www.zmag.org/content/showarticle.cfm?ItemID=2583

WRITE ME

romy@romyshiller.com

ISBN 1425136915

9 781425 136918